ENDORSEMENTS

Throughout the last number of years, I have heard the Holy Spirit say to me on numerous occasions, "The model for what's coming cannot be found in the past, but from the age to come." Clearly there is kingdom truth that we will always build upon as our foundation for the revelation of Jesus Christ. Even so, the Lord is raising up prophetic pioneers who will venture over into the future age and taste the "good word of God and powers of that age to come" and introduce them to the Last Day generation now present on the earth.

That is what Jeremiah Johnson does in this book as he identifies many of the old model systems that we are leaving in order to lay a foundation for the unprecedented yet to come. This will include the unrivaled necessity for humility, contrition, and fervent love for the truth. I love the way Jeremiah values and honors many of the expressions of the Spirit throughout the past while inspiring hope and anticipation for the great new things that will prepare a people for the coming of the Lord. Being a pioneer means cutting a path for others to follow. I greatly value the biblical truth that Jeremiah imparts in this book that will help us navigate these tumultuous days and position a people for divine encounter that will ultimately result in the greatest harvest of souls yet seen. I believe this book will be of great value to those being postured for this purpose.

Paul Keith Davis
WhiteDove Ministries

I attempted to quickly read through *Prophetic Pioneering* by Jeremiah Johnson, but realized immediately that if I wanted to give the revelations and truths contained within the book the attention they deserved, it is definitely not a "quick read"—it is a "deep read." There are many valuable and perspective-transforming selah moments throughout the book that will call you to consider how to prepare for living in this new era. *"Behold, I have put My words in your mouth... to root out and to tear down, to destroy and to overthrow, to build and to plant"* (Jeremiah 1:9-10).

Patricia King
Author, minister, media producer, and host
Patriciaking.com

I am personally impressed with Jeremiah Johnson, who first came to my attention after he publicly apologized for a prophetic prediction that did not come to pass. For that apology, he was attacked by many, but his humility made an impression on many others who found it refreshing, *including me.* As I read his book *Prophetic Pioneering*, it became clear that Jeremiah minces no words about what he believes he is to communicate as a heartfelt message to the Church. He is a gifted communicator who is willing to take risks, who has a passion for God, and who wants to see the Lord have His rightful place in the Church. Regardless of whether you agree with the entire message in this book, I believe you will be challenged to soberly think about what Jeremiah communicates so well.

Rick Renner
Pastor, author, broadcaster
Moscow, Russia

Jeremiah Johnson has given us heaven's perspective of what the Church should look like in this next reformation. As a biblically grounded practitioner—coupled with experiential encounters with Jesus—Jeremiah exhorts the Church toward balance with all fivefold ministry gifts working together, which will result in another great wave of young people being saved similar to the Jesus Movement of the 20th century. This is a powerful and must-read book to add to your collection!

Dr. Joseph Mattera
National Convener of the United States
Coalition of Apostolic Leaders

PROPHETIC PIONEERING

DESTINY IMAGE BOOKS BY JEREMIAH JOHNSON

Cleansing and Igniting the Prophetic: An Urgent Wake-Up Call

Judgment on the House of God: Cleansing and Glory Are Coming

The Power of Consecration: A Prophetic Word to the Church

Houses of Glory: Prophetic Strategies for Entering the New Era

The Altar: Preparing for the Return of Jesus Christ

PROPHETIC PIONEERING

*A CALL TO BUILD AND ESTABLISH
GOD'S NEW ERA WINESKINS*

JEREMIAH JOHNSON

DESTINY IMAGE® PUBLISHERS, INC.
P.O. Box 310, Shippensburg, PA 17257-0310

"Promoting Inspired Lives."

This book and all other Destiny Image and Destiny Image Fiction books are available at Christian bookstores and distributors worldwide.

For more information on foreign distributors, call 717-532-3040.

Reach us on the Internet: www.destinyimage.com.

ISBN 13 TP: 978-0-7684-6370-5
ISBN 13 eBook: 978-0-7684-6371-2
ISBN 13 HC: 978-0-7684-6373-6
ISBN 13 LP: 978-0-7684-6372-9

For Worldwide Distribution, Printed in the U.S.A.
1 2 3 4 5 6 7 8 / 27 26 25 24 23

TO MY WIFE, MORGAN

My last fifteen years of planting churches, ministering around the US and the world, writing books, doing television, birthing ministry schools, and pioneering a global movement would never be possible without you. Your constant love, support, and encouragement over the years have been the greatest blessing of my life. You are a true treasure, inspiration, gift from God, and tremendous wife and mother to our four kids. I earnestly pray that every pioneer in their generation would find a spouse just like you. You truly have made "the road less traveled" feel like I was never alone. Thank you!

With all my heart and affections,

—JEREMIAH

CONTENTS

FOREWORD

Quite a number of years ago I had a dream, and in my dream I heard the Lord speaking loudly; He spoke these words: "Lana, it is not the end of a season, it's the end of an era." In that moment as I woke, I knew that an era was coming when we were going to see God do things we had never seen before. From that day the Lord began to speak to me about the new era that was coming and that we would see God do something completely new (see Isaiah 43:19) and we would enter into unprecedented times. That dream began a journey for me in the secret place with the Lord as He began to reveal His heart to me of things that were to come in this new era, the alignment that He was going to bring in the Church, the deep purifying fire, the cleansing and the shaking that was going to prepare the Church for His glory. The Lord was going to "clean house" and the invitation was essential—to surrender and be "all in" for Jesus, in deep intimacy and friendship with Him, embracing His ways, His strategy, and His blueprint for this new era.

We have now entered that new era. We have entered the time when the majesty and power of God is going to be revealed in such a way that will send shockwaves into the Church, restoring the fear of the Lord, bringing significant alignment, judgment in the house of the Lord, reformation of the prophetic movement, the greatest arising and positioning of His Church in the earth that we have ever seen, and so much more. In this new era, we are going to see pioneering trails, unprecedented pathways, depths of communion with the Lord, oneness with fellow brothers and sisters in Christ that will blossom forth in the earth, birthing and blossoming of the new wineskin that is going to carry His glory. All of these works of God, I believe, require a place of fresh surrender from His people, a humility, and a tenderness toward Him to hear what He is saying, to learn His ways, and to let go of the old and truly embrace the new and make room for Him. Jesus Christ is taking center stage again in this new era and His glory is coming.

The sons of Issachar knew the times and the seasons, and they also knew what Israel ought to do (see 1 Chronicles 12:32). This is not a time to presume or assume what God is doing or going to do in this new era; it's a time to truly seek His heart, to minister unto Him and hear the revelation, the dreams of His heart, His strategy, and His blueprint for this new era. It's a time to arise as His friends in the earth to build with Him in a way that is unapologetic, bold, for His glory, and in His way. That requires us walking in deep friendship with Him to hear and discern what He is doing in this glorious new era.

This incredible book by Jeremiah Johnson is a pathway, a glorious, divine map released from the heart of God to you to encourage you, refresh you, strengthen you, prepare you, and equip you for the days ahead and revelation of many things the Lord is going to do in this new era. From the arising of the New Jesus People Movement to pioneering in the new era to the mantle of Rees Howells to the cry of Evan Roberts, Jeremiah has set the table in partnership with the Lord for you to sit and feast, meditate, prepare yourself, and engage by faith and obedience to what the Lord is speaking for this new era. The revelation that Jeremiah releases in these pages from the heart of God will not only give you greater insight into what God is going to do, but this book also contains the wisdom to know how to position yourself and walk in the revelation that God is releasing.

As I read the pages of this book, my heart was full of gratitude and praise to the Lord that He is God who releases revelation and strategy so we know how to partner with all He is going to do. Jeremiah has been entrusted with these powerful, crucial, and weighty messages from the Lord for the global Church as he walks in deep friendship and communion with the Lord, ministering unto Him. It is my absolute honor to recommend this book to you. This is not a book to read once and put on the shelf. This is a deep well to continue to dive deep into in this new era to hear the heartbeat and voice of the Lord.

Many of you, as you read these pages, your life and your journey are about to come into context. You've been prepared for such a time as this. For many of you, as you read this book the fire He has placed within you will be ignited. For others of you, a new revival fire will be ignited. This book will mark and brand you with the fire of His heart for this new era and like a trumpet, call you deeper into radical surrender, and call you forth into position, for truly the best is yet to come.

LANA VAWSER
Author of *The Prophetic Voice of God*
Adelaide, Australia

INTRODUCTION

In 2013, I sat as a guest in a prophetic conference where a number of highly respected apostles and prophets were ministering. The conference was glorious from beginning to end. The worship was pure and authentic and the speakers shared such deep revelation with the people of God. While the entire conference marked my heart in an eternal way, it was a simple and profound word that one of the apostles shared that shook me and many others that night.

His assignment was a wakeup call to the Church. Although he never announced the title of his message, the statement he repetitiously used that summarized the essence of his message was profoundly offensive and confrontational: "We don't know what we are doing." We don't know what we are doing in worship. We don't know what we are doing in our sermon content. We don't know what we are doing in strategy. We don't know what we are doing in our service flow. We are doing a lot, but we don't know what we are doing.

The message delivered a sweet sting that brought me to a place of repentance and transformation. As a developing pastor, I had found myself leaning in a direction that many leaders found themselves in in that day. We had bought into the idea that our churches should function primarily to draw crowds. We had discovered the secret sauce to protecting our cash reserves. Our ministries were built around convenience, comfort, and popular accoutrements rather than conviction, transformation, and a demonstration of the power of God. That night through many tears and a divine encounter, I vowed to God I would never build a place He wouldn't want to come. And I decided that night that although I was doing a lot, and although I was building something big, I didn't know what I was doing.

Over the last several years, God has graced me to grow in my understanding of what is significant and eternal. I am thankful God rescued me from carnal pursuits and empty destinations. The revelation of kingdom family, the activation of apostolic grace, and a hunger to build something that reflects the culture of the kingdom of God have become my desires. Yet as a leader who travels the earth and has been graced to engage with many pastors, leaders, and believers, I would like to humbly submit that we still don't know what we are doing.

We've learned how to do ministry without prayer. We've discovered how to sing well without worshiping at all. God help the preachers! We have become the products and puppets of people and peer pressure rather than steel-spined prophets who desire to be an oracle of God. We are enamored with crowds and followings but have lost the biblical metric of success. We've entered into dangerous territory where we have exchanged spiritual legacy for numbers, crowds, and cash. And in the midst of this leadership crisis, who or what shall we look to as a model worthy of our attention?

I believe the Church is starving for apostolic leadership that has the ability to be scriptural, authentic, articulate, and fresh. Needed is a blueprint for the Spirit-empowered Church that is anchored in the ancient text of the Bible and breathed upon by the Holy Ghost. We must able to execute and apply the truth of Scripture in a 21st-century context. In order for this to happen, we need a spirit of wisdom and revelation to rest upon the Church. Paul prayed that for the church at Ephesus. I pray it for you! May God remove the scales from our eyes! May He grant that we see with the Spirit and through the Spirit!

In addition to fresh revelation that God is releasing for His people, I believe He is supplying fresh kingdom vocabulary that enables us to speak to our world the things of God and His kingdom. This is the true move of Pentecost! Antiquated terminology, churchy phrases, and Christianese will not be well received or understood in our generation. We need a fresh, Spirit-induced language that articulates the how, clarifies the why, and boldly proclaims the what God is doing in this epoch season. Blueprints that our forefathers built with simply can't be borrowed, copied, and pasted in our day. We need an ear for hearing the word of the Lord, eyes for seeing the plans and purposes of God, and a mouth that can declare with accuracy and unction what God is saying as it regards the advancing of His kingdom in the earth.

It is for these reasons and others that I am grateful for this work written by my friend and brother, Jeremiah Johnson. His heart for righteousness and his passion for the body to become all that God has intended for her to be is refreshing and needed in this hour. Within these pages lies an apostolic blueprint written in a powerful, prophetic, and even practical way. We need to be provoked and encouraged. We need to have articulation and activation. No more just hearing a "nugget" and losing it in notebook nothingness.

What Jeremiah has written is no quick-fix map that takes you from where you are to where you want to be in six easy steps. That would remove the need to lean on the Spirit for His voice and direction. Pioneers don't use maps. Pioneers go where few if any have ever gone. Pioneers will find this book to be more of a compass. It will help you navigate the unknown and unpredictable terrain we find ourselves canvassing in this day. Ultimately, the Spirit will guide us into all that the Father has gloriously appointed for our generation.

BISHOP KEVIN WALLACE
Redemption to the Nations Church
Chattanooga, Tennessee

Chapter 1

The New Jesus People Movement

My personal journey throughout the global pandemic was very different than most. For starters, the church that we planted in Florida in 2010 decided to never close our doors—thanks to a governor who believed in religious liberty and our elder team who was committed to prayer and unity. Second, my ministry travel schedule *increased* during COVID-19, not decreased. To be exact, I traveled and preached in more than 25 states and 45 cities while nearly all of my friends in the ministry were either forced to shut their churches down or were canceled from traveling to speak at conferences and ministries. It was a wild pioneering adventure to be on the front lines of one of the greatest battles the American Church has ever gone through. I saw more miracles, salvations, and deliverances in a two-year period of world crisis than I did the twelve years prior.

My mind is fresh with memories of flying on airplanes with as few as four people on one flight that could sit over 200 and airports that resembled ghost towns on most weekends. The fear in the atmosphere was always tangible except when I would enter into a church or conference that decided to meet during the pandemic. The saints were hungry, courageous, and gave me hope that there was a remnant who grabbed hold of Luke 21:28 (NASB): *"But when these things begin to take place, straighten up and lift up your heads, because your redemption is drawing near."* I often joke and say that if there was one church open in your state during the pandemic, I most likely ministered there!

In my travels in America and at home in our church in Florida, I began to realize throughout 2020 and 2021 that God was up to something significant in our generation. Of course, in no way do I imply God sent the pandemic that has caused suffering for so many, but I understood He was using the global pandemic to help facilitate a desperately needed divine reset in the global body of Christ. I began to experience what I can only describe as the intense groanings of the ending of one church age into the beginning of a brand-new one. I even had an open vision that shook me to the core as I was preaching one night. I began to spontaneously prophesy from the pulpit in April 2020 and said:

> I am releasing cleansing judgment upon the Church because of her pulpit idolatries and the hirelings who have filled My house. For even

now, I am stripping them of their wealth, titles, and desires to be worshiped. Many churches and hirelings will never recover after the virus has lifted because of My judgment. For I will expose the false prophets and priests in the land who feed themselves and not My sheep. Oh, how My heart breaks for the lost sheep who are not being taught how to feed on My word and worship Me. Rather, they are being falsely deceived into man worship, which is idolatry. Repent of celebrity Christianity and recognize the window of time I have now opened for a divine reset in the global Church, says the Lord.

God did not say that the pandemic was judgment upon the global Church. Rather, He was communicating that there was a massive cleansing and revelation during it that He desired to bring to His people in order to prepare us for the future! Man-made church empires are going to continue to fall in the years ahead. Many churches and big-name Christian celebrity preachers will be exposed for

> **"The worship of platforms and ministers has become a stench in God's nostrils."**

sexual immorality, drunkenness, and more. We have not seen anything yet! There is going to be an unprecedented amount of trauma, distrust, and pain inflicted upon this generation of churchgoers. It will be unparalleled. The worship of platforms and ministers has become a stench in God's nostrils. He made a divine decree during the global pandemic that will not be reversed.

While this exposure and judgment on "celebrity Christianity" will bring great devastation on those who are deceived and blinded by pride and arrogance, God's purposes will be revealed. The new breed of pioneers rising in the body of Christ will be mantled with humility, brokenness, and will be highly relational. They will value healthy marriage, family, and servanthood over building their brand and platform. They will be a great refreshing to those who have been hurt and disillusioned by the Church.

House churches and outdoor evangelistic gatherings are going to explode in this new era. Those who attend corporate and local gatherings will hunger for relationship, authenticity, and a true move of God. We are absolutely called to honor the grace and gifting God has put upon leaders, but we must choose to never worship them and commit ministry idolatry again. May God comfort those who are grieving and traumatized by all the church leaders falling and ministry brands being exposed. May God also release hope, vision, and anoint a new breed of pioneers in the earth. The need has never been greater!

I can only speak for myself, but after my open vision in 2020 regarding celebrity Christianity and my travels all throughout the United States during the global pandemic, I began to look past the fear and wave of death. I was constantly asking the Holy Spirit, "What are You trying to reveal and say to Your people? We just cannot go back to business as usual once the virus has lifted! What's next? Wars and rumors of wars? Famine and food shortages?"

The Philadelphia Encounter

As my heart was being deeply stirred by all these questions, I was invited to speak in Philadelphia with a man I had never met before—Ché Ahn. He is the senior leader and apostle of Harvest Rock Church in Pasadena, California. He is well respected in many charismatic circles. I began to pour my heart out to him in the car and he just smiled and listened like a father. After I was done, he put his hand on my shoulder and said:

"Jeremiah, I grew up in Southern California during the Jesus People Movement of the 1970s. During that time, there was a massive shift and transition that God brought to the body of Christ. In one sense, one era in the Church ended and a new one began. It was up to the Church to recognize and discern this. The sooner they began to ask questions concerning their paradigm of church and what God was trying to do in their generation, the sooner they began to catch on and participate with what God was doing."

As Ché uttered these words to me during the pandemic, it was like a lightning bolt struck my inner man. I said,

"That's it! We are in the middle of a New Jesus People Movement in America and the earth. God is using a global pandemic to usher it in, and He is looking for pioneers who are willing to follow His Spirit and transition into a new era. It was grassroots in the 1970s, and the shift God is bringing to the Church in the 2020s and beyond will be grassroots again. God is going to use media, worship, outdoor gatherings, and mass evangelism to radically challenge the methodology of modern-day Church and put an emphasis on healthy family, marriage, and revival."

This father of the faith began to grin and then laugh. "That's exactly right" he said. "And I bless you, Jeremiah, to give language and a blueprint to this generation for what it's supposed to look and feel like.

> **"We are in the middle of a New Jesus People Movement in America and the earth."**

I immediately felt the anointing and confirmation of the Holy Spirit all over my body. In that moment, I heard God say, "The New Era Church is coming, and I want you to write a book about it. I will give you dreams, visions, and revelation from My Word so that you might help pioneer and be a forerunner in it."

If you are hungry for what "next" could look like in the global Church, this book is for you. If you are frustrated, discontent, or even thinking about walking away from the faith, this book is for you. If you are looking for language, confirmation, and a blueprint for the new era, this book is for you. If you are a pioneer, forerunner, and trailblazer, this book will be fuel for your fire and a safe place for you to dream with God.

Saints and leaders, a New Jesus People Movement is upon us! The days of worshiping Christian celebrities and platforms are over. The wineskin of the way church has been done in the earth is quickly fading away, and it's time to shift and transition into a new era. In fact, God is looking for a pioneering people who are willing to go directly to His Word and treasure and model it far above church-growth techniques and marketing strategies. Jesus will be the desire of the nations (see Haggai 2:7). His plans and purposes will not be limited by four walls. He will not allow His glory to fill the empires of men and their religious agendas any longer. He will return for a pure and spotless Bride who has her eyes fixed upon Him. Divine transition is upon us. Let's start walking on this journey together.

CHAPTER 2

PIONEERING IN
THE NEW ERA

Transitions do not often come at desired times in our lives. I know for me personally, whenever my family and I tend to get settled and start growing comfortable, the Holy Spirit finds a way to call us into a pioneering role or new venture. At other times in all of our lives, things happen beyond our control and we suddenly find ourselves having no other choice but to move on into the unknown. In other seasons, our prayers of asking God to do something end up being answered in a way that we did not have a vision for.

To my knowledge, no one had hopes and dreams of a global pandemic in 2020 killing millions of people around the world and causing hundreds of millions to suddenly be thrown into uncomfortable decisions and transitions in their personal, work, and religious lives. In the midst of all the pain, however, many found a gift hidden in the midst of the turmoil. For example, many who once worked long hours outside their home and away from their spouse and family were suddenly forced to work at home underneath one roof. Tens of thousands have testified that God restored their broken marriage and united them with their children due to being confined to one place during the pandemic.

What about the global Church? Millions of Christians around the world had grown accustomed to attending a weekly corporate church service for decades, and in a matter of a few weeks, as the virus spread, it became illegal in most countries to gather with other believers in Jesus' name for almost two years. The United States saw unprecedented attacks on religious liberty never known in the history of America.

What was the hidden gift to the global Church?

A divine reset and transition into a new era. Much like God heard the groanings of the Israelites in Egypt, so God heard the groanings of His people worldwide who have been trapped in the bondages of religion and complacency for decades. I sense prophetically that millions of Christians have now found themselves in the wilderness with a choice. Will we go back to the bondage of religion (Egypt) prior to the global pandemic, or will we follow the Holy Spirit and a new breed of pioneers into the promises of God for the new era?

A Word to New Era Pioneers

In this new era of pioneering beyond the global pandemic, it is impossible to do the will of God without challenging the way things have always been and causing catalytic changes in the body of Christ. This will inevitably cause many to stumble, scoff, criticize, and falsely accuse those courageous enough to dream and lead. The pioneers of the New Jesus People movement will be persecuted by the religious and misunderstood by those holding on to old wineskins. There is a demonic strategy set up against every pioneer in their generation that is not only aimed at destroying them, but also scattering the followers. If satan's attack is successful, everyone involved will come out of the battle hurt and wounded. Remember, satan uses people to attack, criticize, and question pio-

> **"If satan's attack is successful, everyone involved will come out of the battle hurt and wounded."**

neers so that those who are getting set free, refreshed, and empowered by their life and ministry will become confused, disoriented, and altogether stop listening to the emerging pioneers.

Those who lead and dream with bravery cannot allow themselves to become so easily manipulated by people's criticisms and attacks. Pioneers must not try to maintain peace in their heart and life based on whether people accept or reject them. From my own personal experiences, most of the time God will not deliver you from your accusers; rather, He will actually save you by killing the part of you that is vulnerable to the devil by using the accusations themselves.

Visionaries and dreamers must recognize that both God and the devil want them to die, but for different reasons. Satan wants to destroy them through attacks and criticisms and then drain them by their unwavering need to explain themselves and their side of the story. (Please stop wasting your time and energy doing this!) On the other hand, God wants to crucify that part in you that was so easily exploited by the devil to begin with. The rest and peace that pioneers are so desiring in their lives and ministries will only come when they finally die to what people say and think about them.

Pioneers, in order to deliver you from the praise of men, God will baptize you in their criticisms and attacks. It is painful. You will lose many friendships along the way, and the misunderstandings will be many.

You will pay a price that most around you will never see or understand. You are speaking a language of reform and awakening that many in the body of Christ just don't have an eye or ear for yet. Do not grow discouraged, and most of all, do not be surprised when the attacks and criticisms come. Rather than rushing to defend or explain yourself, my advice would be to go before the Lord and ask Him, "What inside of me are You exposing through the accusations and attacks of others that needs to die?"

The New Breed of Pioneers

In an open vision, I saw the spirit of Saul (insecurity and jealousy) operating through church leaders of old wineskins.

It is currently attempting to assassinate a new breed of pioneers who are crazy about the presence of Jesus and absolutely love prayer, worship, and the place of encounter. Pioneers of the New Jesus People Movement won't care who is preaching or leading, so long as God manifests His glory.

I feel deeply compelled by the Spirit of God to speak a father's blessing as a leader in the body of Christ over a new generation of firebrands that understands that the old wineskin of the global Church cannot contain the new wine God is pouring out.

I declare, "You are not rebellious or prideful because you know there has to be more than church programs, three songs, and a nice motivational sermonette. Your concern over many church leaders who have lost the fresh anointing of the Holy Spirit because they have forgotten their first love is justified! Even as your heart has longed to be fathered and given permission to burn for Jesus, do not allow an orphan heart and a spirit of bitterness to grab a hold of your heart. Yes, you are hurting and feel rejection, but as you walk in humility and allow God to heal you, He will use you in the days ahead to do for those you lead that which your fathers refused to do for you."

> **"The old wineskin of the global Church cannot contain the new wine God is pouring out."**

Many of these new breed pioneers and firebrands rising have not been fathered and released like they should have because of the jealousy and insecurity of their leaders, but in the days ahead, they will move in an opposite spirit!

Breaking Free from Religion

One of the most significant shifts taking place beyond the global pandemic is a breaking away from the spirit of religion that has been strangling so many pioneers and forerunners for decades. Where human religious traditions govern church services, everything is scripted, pre-planned, and methodically carried out. There is no room for anything spontaneous, Spirit-filled, or shifting of the service in nature because those actions cannot be controlled or predicted. Religious traditions thrive on what can be controlled, predicted, and expected. These kinds of church services end before they begin because they are robotic and mechanical.

The ministry of the Holy Spirit is the number-one enemy of the religious traditions of men. It brings spontaneity, fresh vision, and unpredictability to church services, which makes the church leaders and saints who operate in a religious spirit very uncomfortable. When worship leaders stop singing the words on the screen and sing a spontaneous song to the Lord, religious traditions are challenged. When men and women of God preach under a strong prophetic anointing that challenges structures and systems, religious traditions become very upset. When saints prepare to participate at corporate gatherings rather than be entertained, religious traditions become afraid.

The unbelievable thing to me is that half the church leaders and saints who reject the types of thoughts I just wrote above actually claim to be "Spirit-filled." The truth is that in many churches we have regulated the ministry of the Holy Spirit to the signs out by our roads, but He hasn't moved in our midst in years! How can we profess to be "Pentecostal" or "Charismatic" while nothing in our church services says so? During my ten years of planting a church and leading corporate service with hundreds of people in Florida, I never once created an "order of service." We never put a single clock in our sanctuary. Our services were never a free-for-all but rather a safe place where the Spirit of God could move with order and edification.

> **"Time restraints and drive-through mentalities will not work in the new era."**

Time restraints and drive-through mentalities will not work in the new era. The sound of glory coming will never be dominated by one man's voice but by a family of believers who are working together in the Sprit with the fivefold ministry. Church leaders and saints will partner together to create houses of glory all over the earth. Fivefold ministers will train and equip the saints for ministry and create environments for the gifts of the Holy Spirit to flow like never before.

Pioneers and Settlers

If God has called you to plant or start a church, move-ment, ministry, business, etc., you have to accept that most people around you are called to be settlers. In other words, they do not like change. They prefer formulas and reliable solutions. They find no glory in blazing new paths and taking big risks. Settlers prefer a fifty-year plan that they will stick to at all costs. Settlers question pioneers at every fork in the road with, "I thought you said..." without realizing it is the courage and bravery of the pioneer that allows them to enjoy the fruit of the new frontier.

I want to encourage pioneers today to not take it per-sonally when the settlers around you just don't know how to rejoice and accept the new venture God has called you into. When you tell them God is moving you geographically, they will question your motives. When God tells you to step out in faith and sow big financially, they will call you a bad stew-ard. When you tell them God has redirected you and the path you are on is no longer the one God wants you on, they will tell you that you are untrustworthy.

You can try to explain to settlers all day long the process of how you got to where you are and it will never be good enough for them, and that's okay. You have to understand that being led by the Holy Spirit looks erratic and is quite frankly tiring to them. The new challenges and financial needs that pioneers find exhilarating to tackle and can't wait to see how God comes through become a major burden and fear for settlers. When you are most excited, they are most likely terrified. Pioneers and settlers are just wired differently. Period. However, we need them both. Faith leads to the occupation of the promises of God and fear leads to rebellion and sin. Pioneers, walk in humility, forgiveness, and honor always. The settlers are your passport to make you learn how to lead with Christlike patience, endurance, and meekness.

Pioneering in Cities and Regions

Pioneers do not look at geographic maps and roll the dice to see where they will land. Rather, they are assigned and sent to specific regions and cities with blueprints from heaven. They frequently rely on divine timing, strategy, and supernatural means of provision, prayer, and fasting to complete the work God has given them to do.

For the pioneer, those territories and cities that produce the most warfare will eventually become the spaces and places of their greatest inheritance. Settling in or backing down are never options for pioneers. They have been divinely commissioned with assignments and strategies from God and will not stop or move onto another city or region until what they have been sent to do has been accomplished.

When pioneers enter into cities and regions with blueprints and a fresh commission from God, power couples whom I call the"Priscilla and Aquillas" will already be waiting for them. (See Acts 18.) These will be marketplace and city gatekeepers with influence and resources that pioneers do not have. They will work together and partner in the kingdom of God. It is so important for pioneers to recognize that they cannot fulfill the will of God simply on their own with a divine commission, but they also need financial resources and city influence that other people have.

Pioneers are also often sent into regions and cities to discover, call forth, and mentor other young pioneers who could not even be aware of the grace on their lives. The seasoned pioneers' "yes" will be what unlocks the DNA for many young pioneering sons and daughters.

Wisdom in Pioneering

Seasoned pioneers have to be careful that they are not so intense and task oriented that they miss their opportunity to father and mother young Timothys that God will send them. Pioneers are often misunderstood because of the prayer burden and God-given passion and focus that they possess. They are frontline soldiers who possess keen prophetic awareness of spiritual darkness that is close by. They grow easily frustrated with groups of people who are lethargic in an hour of crisis.

Pioneers must settle in their hearts that the fruit of their work in cities and regions will often not be fully recognized or honored until long after they have moved on to their next assignment and season. An adequate "thank you" from those they poured out their lives into will never match the sacrifices they made, and this is something that pioneers will just have to accept. Through maturity and many painful seasons, pioneers will ultimately realize that they must obey the voice of God at all costs, not for the applause of man, but because their Father has said so. His affirmation alone must be enough for pioneers.

My Personal Journey

Have you ever been publicly humiliated, misunderstood, falsely accused, lost dear friends, taken significant financial losses, headlined national news articles, and received multiple legitimate death threats as you did your best trying to navigate the leading of God in your life?

2021 was the most difficult, embarrassing, crushing, and yet glorious year in my life. Being a public figure with large online influence drew me right into the center of wave after wave of demonic attacks and also the severe discipline of the Father. Trying to process all that was happening to me both publicly and privately became impossible on my own. I recognized I desperately and urgently needed help!

As a pioneer, leader, and even individual, it is so important to have the self-awareness to know when you have taken arrows between the armor and have been seriously wounded in battle. You cannot continue to fight on your own because now your own discernment has been compromised due to the amount of warfare and crushing of God you have experienced. You will react to people out of your pain and rejection and become toxic in relationships without even knowing it. During 2021, I was literally rescued by four specific people. I am forever indebted to them for running toward me in my greatest season of fiery trial and not abandoning me.

1. Dr. Michael Brown spoke truth in love when I needed it, and it was often. He was committed to not allowing me to play the victim and feel sorry for myself. I remember crying with him in his house as he shared the severe dealings of God in his own public ministry at my age. He wept sharing key lessons from God, and it pierced my soul. His pure, tender, yet fiery prayers and heart for me strengthened my foundation in the Word of God and crushed any pride hiding deep within my heart.

2. Patricia King nursed me back to health emotionally as my heart had become hardened and poisoned due to all the accusation and misunderstanding I had endured from friends and ministry colleagues. Her care for my heart health and phone calls just to see how I was doing washed me in the healing power of Jesus. The timely Scriptures she would send me confronted anger and disarmed lies. She refused to allow me to grow bitter toward the body of Christ. She taught me love and forgiveness in ways I had never known.

3.   Corey Russell was a brother to me who allowed me to talk through my inner struggles in a safe space. I would fly to meet with him in Dallas and spend hours in the prayer room and just hanging out. He constantly encouraged me to find my true self and calling in the midst of the pain and was the intercessor I needed to pull me through. His consistent example of a life of prayer challenged me to the core.

4.   Sherman Dumas was a man I had never met or heard of, yet on July 21, 2021 he broke the power of witchcraft off my life at a public meeting in Pittsburgh and I have never been the same. He felt compelled by the Holy Spirit to spontaneously stand in the gap for how the body of Christ had slandered and maligned me, and heaven answered that day. His prophetic words literally revived my soul and restored my prophetic mantle. It is a day I will never forget so long as I live.

2022 turned into an unbelievable year of God's favor, blessing, and multiplication. It is truly stunning to consider what we have been through and where He has brought us. I could have never dreamed on those dark days in 2021 what He would now ask us to steward and pioneer through The

Altar Global, The Altar School of Ministry, and The Ark Fellowship in Kannapolis, North Carolina.

Pioneers, I do not know what you are going through today. I do not know who has deeply wounded you, betrayed you, or what door you hoped for that has now been slammed in your face. I do not know the depth of your pain, but I can testify that God will use every single trial for His glory and your good *if* you will get low and walk in humility. Die to your need to be right and ask the Holy Spirit to do the deepest work of forgiveness in your life that you have ever known. Hold on to the goodness of God. His love will never fail you.

A new era is upon us, and we need our pioneers and reformers ready to blaze new paths forward in every sphere of society with clean hands and a pure heart. Fresh strategy and divine solutions await this generation of courageous ones. God began to speak to me about the life and ministry of Rees Howells and how his mantle is going to fall in this new era. He was a true pioneer of prayer and surrender who shifted many things in his generation. In the next chapter, we will take a closer look at the legacy he left for all of us.

CHAPTER 3

THE MANTLE OF
REES HOWELLS

Pioneering in this new era will at times mirror and even recapture what some mighty men and women of the past have modeled and paid a dear price for. God began to speak to me concerning Rees Howells and the special invitation He is giving to this generation of pioneers to look back at his life and dig for the treasure he left us. There are certain aspects of his ministry and lifestyle that we must grab hold of if we are to accomplish God's will in the decades ahead of us.

D.L. Moody said, "The world has yet to see what God can do with a man fully consecrated to him." The life of Rees Howells could probably be summed up in this one quote. Rather than being a man who was known for any particular spiritual gift, he was a man who partnered with heaven to change the course of history simply by surrendering every aspect of his life shown to him and staying in constant communion with the Holy Spirit.

Rees was a Welsh man raised in a good Christian home, learning Bible stories from his parents and grandparents at an early age. He was God-conscious and sensitive, not drawn to the things of the world, incredibly generous, and upright. He loved church and prayer meetings and enjoyed a sense of being pure before God. But when a cousin challenged him on whether he was truly born again, he resisted the necessity, feeling that he was probably born with a good nature and never seeing any born-again person around him who lived more upright than he.

One day while hearing a testimony of a Jewish man in church, he had an encounter with Jesus at Calvary that gripped him. The realization of being born into sin, needing to be saved, and Jesus loving him more than any other by dying for him washed over him. He knew in that moment that he did not simply have a mental assent; he had become a citizen of another kingdom.

Soon the Welsh Revival began, and Rees quickly was exposed to the move of the Spirit, which was often accompanied by confession of disobedience and unforgiveness. He encountered the Holy Spirit in a way that may seem very different from today's charismatic encounters. Revelation hit him that the Holy Spirit was a Person who needed a temple of flesh and blood to dwell in. He came to him to take full possession of what Rees had already given to Jesus. The Holy

Spirit would become the Tenant, and he would just be the dwelling place. In Rees' encounter, the Holy Spirit made it very clear that to receive Him meant unconditional surrender. There would be no sharing. His "self" must be given up, his fallen nature must go, and every decision would belong to the Holy Spirit. After five days of weeping and wrestling, he surrendered his life to the Spirit and tremendous joy filled him. But his process of surrender had only just begun.

For decades the Holy Spirit would take Rees through greater and greater levels of surrender, humbling, and unconditional obedience that would continue to result in greater levels of communion and abiding. Increased communion and abiding brought deeper levels of "gaining position" in prayer. No stone could be left unturned in the process of surrender. No thing of this world would be permitted to master him. Food, finances, the fear of man, reliance on man, reliance on self—all had to be radically processed to lose their grip on him. It wasn't about sin; it was about nothing having a hold on him. Public humiliation, repeatedly giving all away, exposure to deadly diseases, and loving the worst of the worst in society were his training

> **"Every request of the Spirit had to be obeyed completely, even if it meant days of wrestling. This was the only path to true surrender."**

grounds to letting his self-nature die and "his Tenant" have full control. Every request of the Spirit had to be obeyed completely, even if it meant days of wrestling. This was the only path to true surrender.

And yet his was not a journey of darkness and depression as one might think. Beyond every agony in the process of surrender was the exhilaration of the joy of freedom. Past every shadow of death was sharing in oneness with the risen Christ. Not only did he become a man free from the entanglements of this world, but one who could live in the place of deep communion and abiding that only those in such surrender can experience. Living this life in the fullness of Christ was beyond comparison.

These processes of surrender and abiding allowed him to "gain position" in the place of prayer. Full surrender meant that no prayers were prayed on a whim, from a need, or left to chance. Only assignments given by the Holy Spirit were taken on, and only the prayers that the Holy Spirit prayed were prayed. Every prayer burden meant that he must first personally walk through the circumstance, identify with the struggle, and overcome in the spirit in order for the person he was praying for to break through. Outcasts, tramps, orphans, and the diseased—he was given those he had no natural love for, that he might bear their burden, gain God's heart, be pulled through, and gain a position of authority.

Obedience and surrender were his focus, not how important the prayer assignment seemed to men. His first

assignment was learning to love, walk with, and pull an out-
cast man through in prayer for three years. After years, the
prayer assignments went from an individual person to the
most hardened, sinful village. Step by step, he had to gain
position. His own comfort was traded in for standing in place
of that person or people. Not one prayer was fulfilled without him first sacrificing in every way. Each process required
the same—deeply abiding with the Lord—which brought
greater cleansing, leading to a breakthrough in him that in
turn secured the victory in prayer. He lived from the prin-
ciple that, "Only so far as we have been tested and proved
willing to do a thing ourselves can we intercede for others."[1]

Each level of surrender brought a new level of victory that
gave authority to conquer the next. Eventually, the position
he had gained in intercession through submission and abiding
were used to bring forth moves of the Spirit internationally.
Through the same process, severe demonic oppression over
villages gave way to the power of the living God. Thousands
were saved and a move of the Spirit would break out wherever
he went. Every small lesson he had learned was now being
used to leverage breakthroughs on a large scale. And yet, as
would become the pattern in his life, the Lord pulled him
out of the spotlight of men and a ministry he loved to raise up
training facilities that focused solely on discipleship. What
became a popular college went through the fire—from in
the spotlight to being hidden, from many to few. Everything
had to be birthed by and depend on God rather than men.

This season caused lectures to cease and a remnant to rise that developed completely in the place of prayer. Little did he know how the Lord would use this season and facility of prayer in the days ahead.

The Lord would eventually turn one training facility into three along with a children's home. Each one was gained in the same pattern of abiding, surrender, prayer, faith, and dependency. Assignments of prayer would come and lectures would be shut down to tend to them. What had once been done by Rees individually was now being produced by young men corporately. They too must now walk the journey that he had walked. This journey of intercession brought the visitation of the Holy Spirit, the exposing of the inner places of their hearts, and the request for complete surrender to these young people just as it had to him. The burden of the work was revealed to them as well as the level of attacks that would come that could never be handled on their own. These encounters with the Holy Spirit would be needed, not simply for themselves but for the world. "The college truly became 'a house of prayer for all peoples.'"[2]

> During the four years previous to the outbreak of World War II...the Lord was changing the burden of Rees Howells from the local concerns...to national and international affairs. As he said, "The world became our parish and we were led to be responsible to intercede for countries and nations." We have also seen how the

Lord was preparing, in the company at the College, a special instrument of intercession for the coming world crisis.[3]

The encounters, surrender, and deep purification led them to the place of becoming a global prayer room amidst the greatest world crisis as a demonized man became set on taking over the world and eliminating the Jewish people. Every position gained and the practice of being hidden in prayer would now be leveraged to gain position on a global stage through specific prayers from the Holy Spirit.

Every prayer and motive was checked to make sure that the Holy Spirit dictated every prayer for each situation. The Holy Spirit would speak of their assignment, "You

> **"The encounters, surrender, and deep purification led them to the place of becoming a global prayer room amidst the greatest world crisis."**

are more responsible for this victory today than those men on the battlefield. You must be dead to everything else but this fight," and, "Don't allow those young men at the Front to do more than you do here."[4] Everything they had gone through had trained them for this moment. For six years the Holy Spirit led this assignment in this way each and every day until it miraculously broke through and eventually the Jews' State of Israel was secured. Though there was great thankfulness for this peace, they declared that their ultimate hope for peace centered around Jesus returning and setting up His kingdom here on the earth. Just a few years later, Rees Howells would go home to be with the Lord, having given everything he had for this final assignment.

The Mantle of Rees Howells

In the new era, I see the Lord raising up men and women like Rees Howells who will be marked with deep relationship with the Holy Spirit that produces radical surrender. This will give birth to a prophetic prayer movement beyond what we have seen, which will decree His global purposes as crisis and darkness continue to rise. As the Lord brings the Church into a new era, the "new wineskin" will include an old mantle being poured out again. Just as God raised up a global prayer movement marked by prophetic prayer through a man who chose to journey with the Holy Spirit into deep surrender and communion, so the Lord will again raise up an end-time prophetic prayer movement with prayers that are proceeding from the mouth of God (see Matthew 4:4). Prayer dedicated by the Holy Spirit will be declared through vessels "on earth as it is in heaven" (see Matthew 6:10). These words of inter-cession will carry power and authority from those who have gone through the purifying fires of surrender into abiding with the Holy Spirit. From this place, great position will be gained in prayer to affect nations, wars, regions, and Israel preceding the return of the Lord.

Deep Relationship with the Holy Spirit

A key mark of this mantle will be the depth of relationship with the Person of the Holy Spirit. Greater levels of relationship will be the foundation to produce greater levels of surrender. Similar to Rees Howells, the nature of this relationship with the Holy Spirit will be a paradigm shift from "hosting an honored guest" to "moving out all of my stuff for the new Tenant to have the entire place to dwell." Rather than just "sharing my things," it will be "Him moving in all of His things." First Corinthians 6:19-20 will become a reality rather than a concept: *"Or do you not know that your body is the temple of the Holy Spirit who is in you, whom you have from God, and you are not your own? For you were bought at a price; therefore glorify God in your body and in your spirit, which are God's"* (NKJV). Our perceptions will change from seeing *ourselves* as the primary dweller of our lives to *Him*.

As this happens, the humanistic and orphan tendencies in us will be confronted. Many today would be offended at the language of surrender that Rees uses of the Holy Spirit's "ownership" of him. This level of submission feels "impersonal" as we are no longer the center of the relationship. But the truth is that as this right perception is restored, a deep communion that is centered on Him (the Tenant) rather than us (the dwelling) will come like we've never experienced before.

The words of Jesus in Luke 22:42 (NKJV), *"Nevertheless not My will, but Yours, be done"* were not simply the words of a slave obeying a master. They were the words of a fully submitted Son who had spent 33 years on earth cultivating deep communion with His Father. Jesus made Himself a dwelling place for the Father to have full residency (see John 5:19; 8:28). And because of this, He walked in the deepest communion with the Father that any man has ever known (see John 17:20-26). The restoration of the Holy Spirit's rightful place in our lives *is* what creates deep intimacy as He is able to fully dwell in us.

This relationship with the Holy Spirit "levels the playing field." Rather than only the specifically gifted minister being used, now every believer who fully surrenders his or her life becomes a conduit of His power. Stephen was an ordinary man who was chosen to serve in practical areas of the Church rather than being selected as a "preacher" or "minister." But his relationship with the Holy Spirit set him apart in such a way that he garnered the attention and anger of the religious system more than the leading preachers and apostles of his day (see Acts 6 and 7)! The Holy Spirit is going to visit "ordinary" men and women in the marketplace, families, schools, and government again. Like Stephen, all those who allow Him to dwell in them in this way will be used for Him to flow through (see Acts 2:17-18).

Many in the past season have only focused on the *actions* of the disciples with the Holy Spirit in the book of

Acts. But in the days ahead the Lord will raise up men and women like Rees Howells who first begin with the foundation of *relationship* with the Holy Spirit that Jesus lays out for His disciples in John 14 and 16. In this place, the relationship with a Person is the pursuit, and the action or gifting is the overflow. God will raise up ordinary men and women who develop deep communion with the Holy Spirit, leading to complete surrender of everything He asks, resulting in extraordinary things being done through them.

Radical Surrender

Like Rees' early years, the concept of the Christian life as simply walking an upright and moral life, having an affinity for God, and even enjoying services and prayer meetings will no longer have relevance in days ahead. The Lord is going to raise a people in the earth who welcome the fires of purification so that they might walk in radical surrender. The Galatians 2:20 (NIV) revelation of *"I have been crucified with Christ and I no longer live, but Christ lives in me"* will go from a nice concept to a way of life.

As true relationship with the Holy Spirit becomes the foundation, radical surrender in the days ahead will reach new heights. No longer will we try as hard as we can to give things up; the very One asking us to every level of surrender will now also be the "main Tenant" on the inside of us to "pull us through." When we are the center and He is the guest, surrender is limited. However, when He is the center,

He is able to be the *"God who works in you to will and to act in order to fulfill his good purpose"* (Philippians 2:13 NIV).

This surrender will be marked with great humility as the pursuit of holiness turns back to being God-centered. Instead the main focus of holiness being "getting rid of all of my junk" (man-centered/humanistic), it will once again focus on making room for the Holy Spirit to make His residence in me. This process will go far beyond sin. Every aspect of self and every care of life that has had its grip on us will be processed to lose its hold. The motivation of "making me better" will give way to "making Him room." As humanism begins to leave our ideology of holiness, a humility will come that is founded on John 3:30—*because* of the fact that He must increase, a burning passion will rise that we must decrease. New desire will come that everything on the inside of us that hinders Him from having "full room" must go. Only when the Holy Spirit is truly in control can radical surrender that is marked with humility be birthed.

An End-Time Prophetic Prayer Movement

Every level of surrender and deepening of relationship with the Holy Spirit led Rees Howells into gaining position in the place of prayer. Not only did authority increase, but so did the prophetic. Surrender and communion meant that not one prayer could be prayed from his own heart and mind. Every word that was prayed could only be *"that proceeds from the mouth of God*" (Matthew 4:4 NKJV). As a result, an entire company was raised up that prophetically decreed the prayers of heaven into the earth amidst global crisis.

In the new era, the Lord is going to raise up many ordinary people, who are radically marked with surrender and relationship with the Holy Spirit, and turn them into a company through which the earth will shake. Comfortable with hiddenness and desiring only for Him to receive the glory, they will form a movement in the earth to rival the plans of the enemy before the Lord's return. They will not simply pray whatever comes to them, but the full takeover from "the Tenant within them" will cause them to declare "*on earth as it is in heaven*" (Matthew 6:10 NKJV).

Businessmen or stay-at-home moms, schoolteachers or grandparents, doctors or politicians—title and occupation won't matter. Radical surrender and submission to the Holy Spirit will be the only qualifying factors to be a part of this end-time praying and pioneering army. Just as the Holy Spirit raised up Rees' school to produce instruments of intercession for the coming world crisis, so these will be raised up to declare His purposes for nations, wars, regions, and the salvation of Israel. As Rees' company had to labor in the place of prayer as hard as those fighting on the battlefield, so this coming company will be conditioned through the purification process to remain in the fight. The days of 30-minute random prayer meetings will become obsolete in the new wineskin as prayer will become specific with the process leading to a Joel 2:28-29 outpouring over this movement. Assignments will be carried and worked on for years as the enemy rages, yet God's purposes prevail.

In the new era, the Lord will shift the global prayer movement into a heavy anointing of the prophetic that will be birthed out of intimacy and surrender. But unlike movements led only by men with great gifts and talents, this will come from those who have been processed in purity, humbled in hiddenness, and surrendered to the Spirit. This place of prayer will become "the great equalizer" as every man and woman from every walk of life who has submitted to the Holy Spirit's process will be able to shake the earth from wherever they are through the place of prayer.

> **"This coming company will be conditioned through the purification process to remain in the fight."**

Notes

1. Norman Grubb, *Rees Howells: Intercessor* (Fort Washington, PA: CLC Publications, 2016), 93.
2. Ibid., 207.
3. Ibid., 231.
4. Ibid., 239.

CHAPTER 4

REVISITING ANTIOCH

ioneering in this new era is going to see apostolic
Christianity found in the book of Acts restored to the
global Church. Specifically, I believe God is highlighting
Acts 13 and the church at Antioch as a prototype for what
must come forth in the decades ahead. It says in Acts 13:1-3
(NASB):

> Now there were prophets and teachers at Antioch,
> in the church that was there: Barnabas, Simeon
> who was called Niger, Lucius of Cyrene, Manaen
> who had been brought up with Herod the tetrarch,
> and Saul. While they were serving the Lord and
> fasting, the Holy Spirit said, "Set Barnabas
> and Saul apart for Me for the work to which I
> have called them." Then, when they had fasted,
> prayed, and laid their hands on them, they sent
> them away.

Paul and Barnabas were sent by the Holy Spirit as apostles from Antioch, and many prophets and teachers resided there. It was a training and equipping center that sent out teams on apostolic assignments and missions. It was an atmosphere where the fivefold ministry operated as a team rather than disjointed from one another. In the new era, we are going to see churches planted in all sorts of different wineskins with the common denominator being that they will embrace team ministry, ministry to the Lord, and seek to equip saints into the work of ministry like never before.

After reporting back to Antioch after his first missionary journey with Barnabas, Paul took another trip to see how the saints were maturing in Christ, this time with Silas, a prophet (see Acts 15:32). It would only be a short time until Paul added Timothy to this team (see Acts 16:1-3). Although called as an apostle to plant churches, Paul was constantly surrounding himself with other fivefold ministers. He recognized the need for the grace of Jesus Christ to be fully present and active on his team.

Fivefold Ministry

Each of the five ministries that Jesus Christ has given to His Church in Ephesians 4:11 (apostles, prophets, evangelists, shepherds, and teachers) has a specific grace that determines their function. For example, Paul says that the foundation of the Church is built upon the apostles and prophets (see Ephesians 2:20). In other words, the two ministries of apostles and prophets carry unique grace to lay the foundation of God's house (Jesus Christ) that evangelists, shepherds, and teachers cannot lay. That is not the grace God has given them. While apostles and prophets are foundation-layers, evangelists, shepherds, and teachers have building ministries. Where in the New Testament do you ever find a pastor or evangelist planting a church? You do not because God has not graced them to do so.

One of the primary issues in the global Church is that we have attempted to plant churches with only teachers, shepherds, and evangelists (building ministries) without the foundational ministries of apostles and prophets. Reaping what we have sown, we now have a global Church that in many places is a mile wide and an inch deep. It looks beautiful on the outside, but the foundation is crumbling because of the way we have chosen to build. When Jesus Christ returns, will He say to us "Well done!" or "What have you done?"

Divine Tension

In 2010, I planted Heart of the Father Ministry in Lakeland, Florida, and pioneered there for a decade. I was 22 years old and my wife and I had just married! We began with only a handful of people and no money. We trusted God each week for His will, and He miraculously poured out His Spirit at our gatherings. He brought some of the finest saints and leaders I have ever had the privilege of working with. In 2016, we purchased a multi-million-dollar facility, and in 2018 I laid hands on a team of fivefold leaders and sent them out to plant a second campus in Winter Haven, Florida. In 2020, I laid hands on our elder team in Lakeland, Florida, to carry on the work of the Lord as my family and I transitioned to North Carolina when God began to shift me into global ministry. Trust me when I say I understand in a very real way the divine tension that can exist because of the grace on church leaders' lives. I have not only pioneered churches, ministry schools, and birthed The Altar Global movement, but I have also preached in more than 400 churches around the US and world to date. My own experiences and the conversations and observations I have had with other church leaders have radically shaped my understanding of fivefold ministry.

If you sat an apostle, prophet, evangelist, shepherd, and teacher down and asked them what God was saying to His Church, each of them would give you a different answer because of the unique grace on their lives. The apostle would say the Church needs more maturity, fathering, discipleship, body of Christ relationships, qualified elders, order, and power. The prophet would say the Church needs more holiness, dreams and visions, gifts of the Spirit, and revival. The evangelist would say people are dying and going to hell! We need to preach the gospel, get people saved, and feed the poor. The shepherd would say that people are hurting and broken and need healing, wisdom, protection, and counsel from the Word and Spirit. The teacher would say that the Church needs to learn the Word of God more for discipleship, accurate doctrine, balance, and maturity. What a beautiful thing it is to have different ministries carrying five different portions of who Jesus Christ is, yet called to work together in unity!

It is a glorious thing when apostles, prophets, evangelists, shepherds, and teachers work together in one community of believers! Functioning together as a team of fivefold ministers does not minimize one another's gifting but maximizes them! The church at Antioch in Acts 13 modeled a new-era wineskin for the first-century Church that God is once again going to use in the 21st-century Church for a new era that we are now entering into.

> **"Functioning together as a team of fivefold ministers does not minimize one another's gifting but maximizes them!"**

The Apostolic and Pastoral

It will be helpful for the reader to understand the difference between apostolic and pastoral leadership so that we can adjust our thinking, which is so often shaped by corporate America models and not what's found in the Word of God. Apostolic leadership carries a vision to mobilize the saints to invade, occupy, and transform their communities and cities. The apostolic thinks *kingdom* before *congregation*. It aims to send disciples outside the four walls rather than providing programs to keep them in. When apostles lead, people are trained as ambassadors of the kingdom in every sphere of society. Apostolic gatherings are springboards into the future.

Pastoral leadership carries a vision to care for and nurture the lives of the flock. The pastoral thinks *need* before *nations*. It aims to protect the wounded and the broken rather than send them on the battlefield hurting. When pastors lead, people grow emotionally healthy and learn how to live a balanced life. Pastoral gatherings are safe places to heal from the past.

> **"A new era is upon us when we are going to see hospitals for sinners and military bases for saints coexist simultaneously underneath one fivefold ministry team in cities all over the world!"**

While the apostolic and pastoral models carry a very different focus and flavor, they will be *married* in this new era of the global Church. We are going to see the fivefold ministry actually work together, not against one another. Antioch models of church are going to explode around the world (see Acts 13). A new era is upon us when we are going to see hospitals for sinners and military bases for saints *coexist* simultaneously underneath one fivefold ministry team in cities all over the world!

The days of apostles and prophets working together with no pastoral help and teaching grace are over! The days of teachers and pastors working together with no apostolic and prophetic input are over. The days of evangelists feeling like they have no real church family and have been banished to the streets are over. A new era in the global Church has begun.

Navigating Change and Conflict

As new-era wineskins are being birthed around the world, there will be a unique shifting, repositioning, and releasing of fresh assignments to many pioneers and reformers. Geographic regions are opening up and new assignments, alignments, and relationships will replace many of those in former seasons. This will inevitably cause great tension, conflict, and potential misunderstanding among leaders and saints. Beware of the leviathan spirit that will specifically attempt to twist words, sow offense, whisper lies in private, and sabotage would-be public kingdom partnerships. Here are five keys to keep in mind when saints and leaders begin to obey the leading of the Holy Spirit in this next season. It will appear messy, but God's glory will be upon it.

1. There can be differences among Christians and leaders that are not rooted in pride, personal ambition, or offended feelings. However, differences can be rooted in spiritual gifts, grace, outlook, burden, mantles, and callings. Separating and identifying

these differences will be very necessary in the days ahead.

2. A strong disagreement among Christian leaders and saints is vastly different from a personal falling out. It is possible to disagree about vision, protocol, ministry style, etc. and not let the disagreement alienate Christian leaders and saints from one another. God is teaching this generation that honoring one another is not based upon agreement but learning how to recognize God's call on someone even when it does not personally benefit us.

3. For some Christians and leaders in this next season, differences can be brought to a resolution by separation. This is/can be healthy. In this scenario, believers resolve to go their own way based on personal conviction, not bitterness, envy, or strife.

4. Differences among Christians do not have to result in two parties walking away from one another quoting Bible verses, using social media to express their pain and blast one another, or gathering other Christians in an attempt to assassinate the character and ministry of another. In these cases, sometimes it is not about who is right and

who is wrong. Different Christian leaders and saints have different callings, convictions, and burdens upon their lives, and that's totally okay.

5. The separation of Paul and Barnabas in Acts 15:36-41 was not a bad thing! This is an example of two great Christian leaders who just didn't see eye to eye on everything and decided to move on. They didn't attack, didn't insult one another, didn't prey on one another, didn't call up other Christian leaders and start a gossip and slander ring. They just kept advancing the gospel.

I deeply sense prophetically that we are about to see many Pauls and Barnabases who have worked together in previous seasons, no longer work together in the new era. God is reassigning and repositioning pioneers, and this is a *good thing!* Many churches, ministries, networks, and nonprofits are about to experience significant conflict and change among staff and leadership in the decades ahead. Navigating through it all in a healthy manner and with heavenly perspective is going to be so important.

May we all continue to stay in prayer and walk in humility, forgiveness, and love toward one another in this new season in the body of Christ.

Spirit of Leviathan

When you are in a pioneering season of transition and have to explain your decision and process to friends, family, and coworkers, beware of the spirit of leviathan that uniquely comes alive to try to twist your words, question your motives, interpret your actions out of context, sabotage relationships, and stir up unnecessary conflict and spiritual warfare.

As leviathan attempts to sow discord, betrayal, and confusion during your transition, you can escape its grasp if you remain humble, gain and maintain clarity in the place of prayer, are quick to forgive, and refuse to partner with offense. Your goal is not to try to convince and persuade everyone you know what God has spoken to you. The truth is that some are actually committed to misunderstand and question your every move.

> **"You must simply obey God and allow Him who knows the thoughts, attitudes, and motives of your heart to defend you."**

You must simply obey God and allow Him who knows the thoughts, attitudes, and motives of your heart to defend you. He will see you through this season of your life. Leviathan cannot win and will only attempt to bully and intimidate you so long as you hold on to your pride, which is the open door the spirit needs to operate. Shut it down in Jesus' name!

A Blueprint for the New Era

During the month of March, 2022, we celebrated our one-year anniversary at The Altar Global. It had been two years since we handed off the church we planted, Heart of the Father Ministry in Florida, to our elder team and moved to North Carolina. I was enjoying traveling, writing, establishing our global movement, and discipling marketplace leaders through The Altar School of Ministry. In March, I felt specifically prompted by the Holy Spirit to take 30 days off from ministry travel, going into the office, and being on social media to simply wait on Him in worship, fasting, prayer, and adoration. It was so refreshing and encouraging, to say the least. During my time of seeking God, one of my primary questions was, "Is there anything You want to add or take away from what You have called us to build after our first year of birthing and building?"

As many know, The Altar Global is a growing movement of Christians from around the world who share a common urgency and desire for the return of Jesus Christ and the preparation of the Bride for that glorious day. The Altar School of Ministry, which is available online and in person in North Carolina, is where we actively train and equip business owners, marketplace leaders, and students with the message of the return of Christ and the need to prepare the Bride and win souls. We also host several national Altar conferences every year where we invite saints and leaders from all over the

United States and world to gather underneath an anointing for the end times. Our movement is supported and funded by a family of monthly partners, from around the US and world, who sow financially, get discipled through our school, and are profoundly impacted at our national gatherings.

Shock and Awe

One night in March as I was in prayer, I received an unexpected text message from a pastor in our city. He asked to meet with my wife and me. As we sat with him in his office the next day, he shared that God was undeniably leading him to join his spiritual father for a new ministry assignment in another state. *He believed God had spoken to him that he was to offer us his 13-acre church property in our city for absolutely free over a period of three years.*

My wife and I sat stunned. The building was six miles from our home. As we began to walk the campus the following week and cry out to God for clarity, we felt the confirmation of the Holy Spirit all over this offer. First of all, it was one that we had not searched for in any way, and second, his offer to us was not only incredibly generous but was in alignment with numerous prophetic words we had received personally and from leaders around the world. We had outgrown our headquarters after just one year and were waiting on God for our next step in the secret place.

As we began to celebrate God miraculously providing a 13-acre campus for The Altar Global and The Altar School of Ministry, there was something more that the Holy Spirit began to whisper to our hearts.

"Jeremiah and Morgan, I want you to build a modern-day Antioch. (He literally gave us 13 acres and the church at Antioch is found in Acts 13.) I want you to establish a local expression for healthy marriages and families called The Ark Fellowship, and I also want you to continue to lead The Altar Global and teach at The Altar School of Ministry to help America and the nations prepare for the Second Coming of Jesus Christ."

The Ark Fellowship exists to serve families, marriages, and individuals on a local level in their pursuit of God in the greater Charlotte region. The three core values God has given us to rally around are: *Fire, Family, and Fathering.*

I am the apostolic leader of The Ark Fellowship in the pioneering years while I lay Jesus Christ as the foundation of our lives and church, cast vision, disciple leaders, and steward all that He has entrusted to us. I do not anticipate that I will be leading this local expression long term. Rather, as I successfully did in Florida at Heart of the Father Ministry, I will eventually lay hands on a team of elders whom I disciple and commission them to shepherd the flock together as a fivefold ministry team.

The Culture of an Antioch Model

At The Ark Fellowship, we want to create a *culture* that reflects a *kingdom value system*. I will refer to this as "kingdom culture." It is important that we all understand and agree to honor these values so that each facet and department of the church is in harmony and unity with one another. Even more important is that we all do our best by God's grace to model and live out these kingdom values in our own lives, marriages, and families. Below are our five values that we want to build and rally around as a community of believers. I have taken the time to list them and provide a brief explanation so that those who are called to plant churches and establish ministries can see how I have pioneered and grasped God's design for the New Testament Church.

1. We desire to build relationally.

When Paul instructed Timothy in the selection of church leaders, he said, *"Do not be hasty in the laying on of hands, and do not share in the sins of others. Keep yourself pure"* (1 Timothy 5:22 NIV). In 1 Thessalonians 5:12 (AMPC) he said to *"know those who labor among you."* Jesus Christ, the Son of God, came in the form of a man and built relationships with His disciples that led to the gospel of the kingdom spreading to Judea, Samaria, and the ends of the earth.

In the kingdom of God, there will always be areas of need and service. However, we want to create a value system where *relationship leads to service* not *service leads to relationship.* In orphan culture, people are seen as objects and dehumanized in order to use them to get what we need done. In kingdom culture, people are seen as real human beings who have emotions, struggles, and are valued for who they are. Orphan culture thrives on performance and "the show must go on" mentality. It seeks out the most gifted and talented individuals who, oftentimes, are attempting to use ministry to find their own worth, value, and significance. Kingdom culture thrives on relationship, whereby we become a family in which all contribute to the needs of the community as they come. Kingdom culture refuses to sacrifice its DNA of relationship and family to meet every need and demand of those attending.

For example, a church worship team is needed for a church plant. In kingdom culture, we make relationship the foundation for playing on the team, not who is the most talented or who wants money to play at their next "gig." In kingdom culture, the worship pastor will have to find ways to facilitate relational gatherings that *do*

> **"Kingdom culture refuses to sacrifice its DNA of relationship and family."**

not involve playing on a platform. In orphan culture, we plug musicians and singers into a Sunday morning circus where they perform for the attending guests. In kingdom culture, a family of worshipers emerges and learns how to minister to the Lord and His people out of love for one another and the family of believers they are called to lead.

For example, a kids' church is needed for a church plant. In kingdom culture, we ask parents to involve themselves in the discipleship process of their own children and the children of their friends. In orphan culture, we hire or plug in random workers we have no relationship with to fill positions to "babysit the kids." The kids' church pastor will have to find creative ways to build community and family with parents and kids' church volunteers outside of services because, again, human beings are not objects we use to get done what needs to be accomplished. As we invest in people relationally, service together in God's kingdom becomes a natural overflow of our friendship and our love for one another.

As The Ark Fellowship is planted and needs of service arise, we must *first* seek out those we *already* have relationship with. It is also important that we evaluate the quality of relationship we think we really have with the people we already know. Is it based on ministry or genuine friendship? For the new people we do not know who desire to serve, we must be very careful that we do not create orphan culture where we are simply recruiting people to fill vacancies devoid of any relationship.

In kingdom culture, new volunteers are asked to first join the church family, get to know our values, build relationships with department leaders and pastors, and *then* be given an opportunity to serve. Love and relationship must come first, not the other way around! We must heed the words of Paul to know those who labor among us and not be hasty in giving people positions of leadership whom we really do not know.

2. *We desire to build morally.*

As the early Church grew in number and needs arose among the people, instructions were given to *"choose from among you seven men with good reputations [men of godly character and moral integrity], full of the Spirit and of wisdom, whom we may put in charge of this task"* (Acts 6:3 AMP). When deacons (servants of God's people) were chosen, they were required to:

> *...be dignified, not double-tongued, not addicted to much wine, not greedy for dishonest gain. They must hold the mystery of the faith with a clear conscience. And let them also be tested first; then let them serve as deacons if they prove themselves blameless. Their wives likewise must be dignified, not slanderers, but sober-minded, faithful in all things. Let deacons each be the husband of one wife, managing their children and their own households well. For those who serve well as deacons gain a good standing for themselves and also great confidence in the faith that is in Christ Jesus* (1 Timothy 3:8-13 ESV).

For elders, the requirements were even a higher standard. First Timothy 3:1-7 (ESV) says:

> *If anyone aspires to the office of overseer, he desires a noble task. Therefore an overseer must be above*

reproach, the husband of one wife, sober-minded, self-controlled, respectable, hospitable, able to teach, not a drunkard, not violent but gentle, not quarrelsome, not a lover of money. He must manage his own household well, with all dignity keeping his children submissive, for if someone does not know how to manage his own household, how will he care for God's church? He must not be a recent convert, or he may become puffed up with conceit and fall into the condemnation of the devil. Moreover, he must be well thought of by outsiders, so that he may not fall into disgrace, into a snare of the devil.

In kingdom culture, there is a clear standard of morality according to the Scriptures that leaders and those who serve are required to live by. We do not walk in purity with the motivation to be seen by men but rather to humbly please our Father in heaven. In orphan culture, gifting, charisma, and even need is valued over morality. It overlooks

> **"People will always best receive correction through relationship."**

character flaws and red flags in order to keep the ministry machine going. While no one is "perfect," those who desire change and genuine repentance will bear forth tangible fruit in their lives. Building relationally will help to make sure we are also building morally. People will always best receive correction through relationship.

At The Ark Fellowship, we not only want to establish a relational model of kingdom culture but also one where there is a clear standard of morality. As staff and leaders, we need to make sure that our own personal lives and families are in alignment with these values. We cannot ask of people what we ourselves are not willing to submit to. We also cannot call a generation of young people (kids, youth, and young adults) to holiness and righteousness when our own kids living in our homes are not living godly lives.

For example, in kingdom culture, my role as the worship pastor, media, kids, youth pastor, etc. is not only to ask those serving on my team to commit to walking in a relational context together but also a moral one. This will require hard conversations, sometimes awkward questions, and a commitment to honor the Word of God in all we do and say.

3. *We desire to build generationally.*

The promises in the Old Testament were from the God of *"Abraham, Isaac, and Jacob."* Every true revival must span *three* generations. The blessing was, *"to you, your children, and your children's children."* At The Ark Fellowship, we want to model generational blessing in all that we do and say. We want each church department that we build to be a reflection of multiple generations serving together for the work of the gospel and edification of the saints. God spoke to me years ago and said, "Only hanging out with people your own age is a form of self-worship."

For example, we desire to have a worship team that spans multiple generations. We don't want a bunch of millennials only leading us in worship every service. We want to see greeters and volunteers from all demographics and generations. We want to find ways to make sure our kids, youth, young-adult, and older-saints gatherings can work together to serve one another at times. Can the young people go on a Saturday to clean up the yard of an elderly couple? Can the older folks open up their homes to the youth for a cookout?

4. *We desire to build biblically.*

The Ark Fellowship is being planted by Jeremiah and Morgan Johnson. Their role will be apostolic in nature as they have a primary mandate from God to make sure Jesus Christ is laid as the foundation of the church, teach strong doctrine, cast vision, push darkness in the region back, disciple leaders, win souls, and pioneer in the years ahead. As they function in this capacity, they will begin to identify a team of people who have been tested through relationship and servanthood. At the right time, this group of people will be ordained and have hands laid on them as deacons at The Ark Fellowship. These men and women will have the responsibility of functioning as servants of the people in various capacities and responsibilities.

Over time, some within the deacon group will be identified as those who could potentially be elders of the flock in the future. There will be a process during this time where Jeremiah will begin to disciple these couples into the roles and responsibilities of biblical eldership and prepare them to shepherd God's people.

Once the elder team has been approved, Jeremiah will lay hands on them and ordain them into office. There are only two "offices" in the New Testament, which are deacons and elders. As this process becomes complete, a final step will be taken where Jeremiah will begin shifting his focus from pioneering locally to an apostolic oversight role of the elder team and The Ark Fellowship. Once this happens, Jeremiah will be given liberty to focus on travel, writing, and overseeing the church. He will be relieved of the primary leading role he operates in during the pioneering years of the church plant.

In the New Testament, apostles and apostle/prophet teams planted churches, spent the early months and years laying the foundation, discipling leaders, etc. and then laid hands on elder teams who were then responsible for the daily affairs of the local church. Apostles then traveled back and forth and stayed relationally connected to what they had birthed and established.

5. *We desire to build generously.*

The Ark Fellowship is a house where kingdom generosity will not only be demonstrated but taught. When Malachi the prophet began to rebuke Israel for their lack of giving, he said, "You have robbed God of both the tithe *and* offering." In other words, in a culture of kingdom generosity, people are not only expected to tithe but *also* give alms and offerings to the poor, missionaries, and traveling ministers. In Matthew 8, Jesus Himself sat directly across from where the people gave to God and took note of the exact amount they sowed. Clearly, God not only sees what we give but He also measures what we give by how much money we make. We must remember that we are never more like Christ than when we are forgiving and giving.

While sowing generously with our time and talents is also necessary and expected in the kingdom of God, there is no substitute for being good stewards of the finances God has placed in our hands. In kingdom culture, we embrace the words of Jesus: "It is better to give than receive." We will encourage our church family to sow extravagantly into missions, ministers, the poor and needy, and various projects that God lays upon our hearts.

In orphan culture, there is no value of living a blessed life and people therefore become takers rather than givers. In kingdom culture, people are hardworking and blessed. In orphan culture, people are lazy, assume the role of the victim, and constantly beg for help. We expect those who are on staff, who volunteer, and who serve in different leadership capacitates to lead the way in generous giving. The Ark Fellowship believes

> **"Our finances never become eternal until we sow them into the kingdom of God."**

that our finances never become eternal until we sow them into the kingdom of God. May we develop a culture of generosity that is fueled by a value system and kingdom revelation that God desires to do abundantly more than we can ask for or imagine (see Ephesians 3:20).

New Wineskins for a New Era

I wanted to share with you, the reader, my own journey and process as a pioneer for the last fifteen years so that you do not think what I am writing is just theory. I would highly recommend my book *Houses of Glory* for those interested in learning more about the practical steps of church planting, church government, and the fivefold ministry. From successfully planting churches, discipling fivefold ministry teams, birthing ministry schools, and establishing a global end-time movement—we are actively and practically involved in everything that is written in this manuscript.

CHAPTER 5

APOSTLES AND PROPHETS

In Ephesians 2:20 we discover that the ministries of apostles and prophets are foundational in the building of God's house. They have been graced by the Holy Spirit to reveal and unveil the foundation and cornerstone of the Church, who is Jesus Christ. He is the precious and costly stone that Isaiah prophesied about. Surely anyone who puts their trust in Him will not be shaken (see Isaiah 28:16). Apostolic ministry carries a unique burden to see Christ formed in the lives of the saints and for them to be presented to Him as mature, not lacking in anything (see Galatians 4:19). Prophetic ministry carries grace to proclaim the supremacy of Christ and the knowledge of who He is (see Revelation 19:10). True prophetic ministry confronts vain imaginations concerning who God is (see 2 Corinthians 10).

Paul says in First Corinthians 12:28 (NASB), *"God has appointed in the church, first apostles, second prophets, third teachers, then miracles.*" Why are the ministries of apostles and prophets mentioned as first and second? The answer is not because the fivefold ministry is a hierarchy, but rather these two precious ministries are foundational and must be the ones who not only pioneer but engineer the house of God. They have been graced with blueprints concerning how the living stones are to be gathered and built up into an eternal dwelling place for the Holy Spirit (see 1 Peter 2:5).

There is a spirit of revelation concerning Christ Jesus and His eternal plans for His Church that apostles and prophets possess that the ministries of teachers, pastors, and evangelists do not. This reality does not make them better than the others but rather reveals their specific grace and function in the building of God's house. The grace on each ministry will determine the function of all five of them. Modern-day apostles are graced to reveal the apostolic nature of Jesus Christ who is the Chief Apostle (see Hebrews 3:1). Another way to say it is that Jesus is the big "A" and all other apostles that have come after Him are little "a's." No apostles appear in the Bible before Jesus Christ because true apostleship first requires sonship.

Much of apostolic and prophetic ministry in the 21st century is not centered on Jesus Christ and revealing His eternal mysteries to His Church. It is focused on titles, self-promotion, making money, and growing popularity. There are many pastors, teachers, and evangelists who reject apostolic and prophetic ministry for these reasons and they rightfully do so. I am just as concerned with the amount of vanity and carnality in the current apostolic and prophetic movements as I am burdened for those who refuse to embrace apostolic and prophetic ministry. We must return to pure and simple-hearted devotion to Jesus Christ. We desperately need the fullness of who He really is rightly represented in the Church today (see Ephesians 4:19).

The Diotrephes Warning

It is so sad to see how many individuals who claim to be modern-day apostles believe that they carry some form of elitism, superiority, or special privilege from God that His people or the other four ministries do not. If apostolic ministry is properly understood, true apostles recognize that they are servants of Christ and often find themselves enduring intense persecution and suffering (see 1 Corinthians 4). They are uniquely graced to be patient with the weak and demonstrate the humility of Christ in profound ways. Apostles are called to work with teams and serve the body, not operate in arrogance and control.

> **"We must return to pure and simple-hearted devotion to Jesus Christ."**

Third John 1:9 warns of a leader named Diotrephes who loved to have first place in all things. His leadership style was characterized by five main realities:

1. He loved to have preeminence amongst the brethren and in the church.

2. He would not welcome and receive other gifted apostles or traveling ministries.

3. He spoke against other ministers and ministries with malicious words.

4. He forbade those who followed his leadership from receiving and following any of the other ministers and ministries.

5. He excommunicated anyone under his leadership who embraced outside/other traveling ministers and ministries.

I'm convinced there are way too many churches, networks, and ministries around the world being governed by a "Diotrephes spirit" rather than the Spirit of God!

We not only need apostolic order to return to the Church so that Jesus might take preeminence in all things, but we also need so-called "apostles" who are building their own kingdoms and ministries to repent and step aside. The problem with much of our contemporary apostolic ministry is that it brings a "takeover" mentality to the Church in which so-called "apostles" build cult-like followings after themselves.

As mentioned above, they operate in a Diotrephes spirit and want first place in all things (see 3 John 1:9). This is a tremendous tragedy because apostles are the ones who actually carry the grace to connect the body to our true head, Jesus Christ.

Apostles Are Emptied of Themselves

A servant attitude in true apostles will be noticeably natural and sincere. They will not sit on thrones, be worshiped by men, demand honorariums, or walk in a spirit of elitism and entitlement. Apostles are not full of themselves, but rather emptied of themselves! Like Christ, they will readily declare to their audience, "I have not come to do my own will, but the will of *Him* who sent me" (see John 6:38).

The authority that apostles carry is delegated authority. It is given to them because they have laid aside whatever authority they thought was their own to receive the authority of Jesus Christ. True apostolic authority is always recognized and never demanded. It rests properly upon those in submission to authority.

Apostles do not live for themselves, but for others.

"True apostolic authority is always recognized and never demanded."

They do not represent themselves when they speak, but Christ. Apostles fully and completely represent Jesus because they have faced and experienced the death of self, which brings them to a place of being submitted, yielded, and humble servants of/to the body of Christ.

In an age when many of our modern-day "apostles" are inaccessible, demand to be treated like Hollywood celebrities, and are full of themselves, God is raising up authentic apostles who know suffering and persecution well, love to wash feet and serve, and walk in a sweet humility that refreshes everyone they meet.

True Apostles Are Emerging

An apostle is always thinking of you, praying for you, and longing to see you with the affection of Jesus Christ. Their heart is with you! They are joyful over you and at the same time deeply burdened for you concerning your growth in Christ (see Galatians 4:19; Philippians 1:8; Colossians 1:9).

For three years in Ephesus, Paul never ceased personally warning and exhorting the elders of the church, night and day, and with tears (see Acts 20:31). And when he met them at Miletus to bid them a final farewell, they all *wept* as they embraced and kissed him (see Acts 20:37-38). They loved Paul and knew in him they had a true father who loved them.

This is what apostolic fatherhood is all about. We must stop settling for cheap networking schemes and marketing traps to satisfy the ache in this generation for true apostolic fathering.

Do you claim to have an apostle? When is the last time they wept over you as you felt their father's heart for you deep down inside your spirit? I know people claiming to have an "apostle" who can hardly get a phone call with them or one meeting every three months. But they do pay a monthly fee to rent their "apostle's" name so they can feel safe and "covered."

Do you claim to be an apostle? Are you just collecting people's money and building your network, or are you actually involved in authentic relationships with your sons and daughters and praying for them night and day? In fact, there are some apostles who travel so much and blow in and out of every city that, the truth is, it's impossible for them to truly father anyone because they just don't have the time or energy.

I'm convinced that true apostolic fatherhood is going to be restored in this generation. Fathers will invest into sons and daughters for *free* because it's their delight and highest privilege in life. There will be apostolic fathers choosing not to travel so much because they realize they will have a far greater impact staying home and discipling the next generation rather than blowing in and out of the next conference to make a quick buck.

There will be apostolic fathers in the new era who are accessible and modeling what a great marriage and child rearing should look like to the next generation. I'm so excited for the reformation that is coming to the apostolic movement, but it will only come through uprooting and tearing down carnality and deception before the building and the planting can take place. It's going to be a challenge, but true apostolic fathers were made for this. Now is the time for the true apostles to emerge.

Apostolic Christianity

As I continue to search the Scriptures and seek God in prayer, I'm now more convinced than ever that apostolic Christianity is the only wineskin that can host the new wine that God is pouring out in this generation. Denominational structures and the institutional nature of them will continue to hinder and, in most cases, altogether quench the spirit of revival and awakening that is coming upon the body of Christ.

I believe a generation of Martin Luthers (reformers) is going to revolt against denominations and religious structures and form a wineskin of apostolic Christianity that will host the new wine being poured out.

Many of these leaders carrying this type of Martin Luther reformation anointing are currently referred to as "pastors, teachers, and evangelists" within their denominations and religious structures because there is no revelation or embrace of apostles, prophets, or apostolic Christianity. Many of these church leaders know that God has called them as an apostle or prophet and is releasing them to teach apostolic Christianity straight out of the Gospels and the book of Acts (and not from a church-growth text book), but they are unsure concerning what will happen if they make the shift. God is going to strengthen them with the power of His might and confirm His word.

The Holy Spirit has been specifically highlighting to me five states—Texas, North Carolina, Alabama, Tennessee, and Mississippi—as states where reformation is about to take place within denominations and religious structures. The religious spirit is going to attack, accuse, and operate in political games like never before, but the Spirit of God is going to oversee this entire paradigm shift and reformation as apostolic Christianity is restored to the Church.

Remember, in 1517 Martin Luther nailed the paper containing his 95 theses to the church doors in Wittenberg. All he sought was a debate, but

> "We are talking about a fire that is going to burn through denominations and religious structures in the new era."

little did he know he was starting a fire that would burn through the ages! The language of "apostolic Christianity" is more than a debate; we are talking about a fire that is going to burn through denominations and religious structures in the new era.

Ten Earmarks of Apostolic Ministry

1. *They represent Christ.*

The Greek verb is *apostello*, which means "to send forth with a divine commission." An interpretive meaning of the term *apostle* is "one who has been sent forth with a specific, divine commission, *to represent the one* who has commissioned them." True apostles have no interest in representing themselves and their ministries to the public. They are sent into regions and territories to represent Jesus Christ and demonstrate His kingdom.

2. *They are called by Christ.*

In Galatians 1, Paul explains with clarity how he was called by *Jesus Christ* to be an apostle. He received the gospel through a revelation of *Jesus Christ* (see Galatians 1:12). He goes on to say God "*was pleased to **reveal His Son in me***" (Galatians 1:15-16 NASB). Paul had no desire or interest in being called an "apostle" by anyone or anything. None of that mattered to him because Jesus Christ Himself had called him to be an apostle.

3. *They build on Christ.*

True apostles will not build upon any other foundation than *Jesus Christ*. To "align" with an apostle is to submit yourself to a radical pursuit of a revelation of Jesus Christ. Apostles will not and do not plant and build churches upon themselves or their ministry gifts. Rather, they plant churches upon a revelation of Jesus Christ. True apostles seek to remove any unnecessary attention from themselves in the planting of churches and ministries. Apostles establish the authority of Christ by setting in elders and deacons.

4. *They preach Christ.*

Paul continued to explain his apostolic calling in Galatians 1:15-16 (NASB) as he said, "[God] *was pleased to reveal His Son in me so that I might preach Him among the Gentiles.*" He proclaimed to the Corinthians that "*I have resolved to know nothing...except* Jesus Christ *and He crucified*" (1 Corinthians 2:2 NIV). To the church at Philippi he said, "*I count all things to be loss in view of the surpassing value of knowing **Christ Jesus my Lord***" (Philippians 3:8 NASB). True apostles continually preach *Jesus Christ*. Apostolic preaching is the preaching of *Jesus Christ*. True apostles constantly preach on the life, death, burial, resurrection, ascension, and second coming of Jesus Christ. When apostles finish teaching and preaching in regions and cities, the worship and exaltation of Jesus Christ explodes in the hearts of sinners and saints alike.

5. *They manifest Christ.*

True apostles manifest *Jesus Christ* in the earth through extraordinary acts of humility and meekness. They are not title oriented. They have no need for public recognition, only that Jesus Christ Himself receives all the glory and the praise. Apostles take the true authority that they have been given and manifest the gentleness and humility of Jesus Christ (see Matthew 11:29). Apostles are foot washers and bondservants (see 1 Corinthians 4:9-14).

6. *They are fools for Christ.*

True apostles are mocked and slandered. They do not have entourages and mass followings. When they preach Christ, there is either revival or riot. Apostles are not greedy because they continually seek to magnify Christ and give away their possessions to the poor. "We are fools for Christ's sake, we are weak, we are without honor, we are hungry, we are thirsty, we are poorly clothed, we are roughly treated, we toil with our own hands" (see 1 Corinthians 4:10-11).

7. *They are reviled for Christ.*

True apostles are persecuted and continually asked to endure for the sake of Christ. Their focus on Jesus Christ continually causes them to be despised by others who would rather emphasize other subjects in the kingdom of God. Apostles are consumed with laying Jesus Christ as the foundation of the church, and the religious spirit hates this pursuit. Apostles are continually rejected because they will not build on any other foundation than Jesus Christ (see Ephesians 2:20; 1 Corinthians 4:13).

8. *They are fathers in Christ.*

True apostles carry and possess the Father heart of God for His children. They do not father according to their own desires, but they father *in Christ Jesus*. As Paul stated, "*In Christ Jesus I became your father*" (1 Corinthians 4:15 NASB). The life source of true apostles

> **"True apostolic fathering is centered upon the person and work of Jesus Christ."**

who father sons and daughters is *Jesus Christ!* Finding young people who can do your bidding and then calling yourself an apostle is not fathering. True apostolic fathering is centered upon the person and work of Jesus Christ.

9. *They are miracle workers for Christ.*

True apostles minister in signs, wonders, and miracles. As Paul said, *"Truly the signs of an apostle were wrought among you in all patience, in signs, and wonders, and mighty deeds"* (2 Corinthians 12:12 KJV). Apostles carry authority over demons, principalities, sickness, and disease.

10. *They possess the character of Christ.*

True apostles carry the DNA of Jesus Christ inside their being. They understand that in order to be first, they must be last. They recognize that in order to be the greatest, they have to get in the back of the line. True apostles embrace the upside-down kingdom that Jesus Christ taught. In the words of Paul, "we apostles are the scum of the world" (see 1 Corinthians 4:13). True apostles are filled with the fruit of the Holy Spirit. Apostles are not prideful, arrogant, and lovers of money. They do not itch the ears of the carnal but rather preach the truth in love.

It is for these ten biblical reasons above that I personally believe that many who self-proclaim to be "apostles" or are being called "apostles" by others are not, in fact, true apostles. Some of them are evangelists and prophets at best, but many of them do not bear even two or three of the biblical markings explained above. While I firmly believe in the modern-day ministry of apostles, we must go back to the Scriptures so that true apostolic reformation can take place. We must have a generation of apostles who are absolutely possessed, captivated, and fascinated with the Person and work of Jesus Christ. We must have mass repentance among those who are claiming to be "apostles" and are not. May God use the emergence of true apostles in the new era to sound the alarm and set a new precedent in the body of Christ.

The Prophets

New Testament prophets bring forth the testimony of Jesus Christ (see Revelation 19:10). They are not limited to simply encouraging and comforting the body of Christ as found in 1 Corinthians 14. Along with bringing strength and edification to the saints, they are also graced to be confrontational at times, as demonstrated by Jesus Himself in Revelation 2 and 3. Their words will often bring necessary rebuke and correction and should always be given in brokenness and with humility. A.W. Tozer understood this when he wrote and said:

> The words of true prophets are not harsh for the sake of being harsh; they speak words necessary for God to finish His work. God cannot build until He tears down. He cannot plant until He roots up the evil and self-seeking ways of men. He cannot and will not sully His ways with the

methods of men; the overlooking of sin to popu-
late their churches and accomplish their agendas.
He must tear down the lofty pursuits of those
who seek the preeminence in His house.[1]

Five Earmarks of Prophets

1. Prophets are committed to consistently evaluating
and critiquing man-made structures and religious traditions
out of a deep love for God and for His Church. A true prophet's ministry will appear at times confrontational and critical
of existing church structures that have become or are becoming obsolete, irrelevant, and a great hindrance to the Spirit
of God.

2. Prophets are a blessing to apostles and help them from
becoming rigid, legalistic, controlling, and authoritarian.
Prophets are called to keep apostles from functioning from
the position of the "letter that kills" and move them to the
place of "the Spirit that gives life." Prophets must work closely
together with apostles so that blind spots can be revealed.

3. Prophets are protectors of the Church from unhealthy
and unbiblical control that will constrict movement and
hinder growth. Prophets believe that the Church is a living
organism, not an organization, and they will tangle with
church leaders who constrict the freedom of the Holy Spirit.

4. Prophets carry grace to expose false prophets and specifically warn the Church of those voices who tell people
living in sin that God is at peace with them. True prophets

lament over those who use their gifting in order to benefit themselves for carnal desires and sordid gain.

5. Prophets are the eyes of the body of Christ. They help the global Church "see" what is coming and feel deeply moved to prepare themselves and others for the days ahead. True prophets live ahead of their time and are plagued by constant frustration that the people around them have not partnered with the revelation they are releasing.

The Training of Prophets

Receiving the capacity as prophets of God to minister prophetic words that correct, rebuke, uproot, and tear down is no small matter in the sight of God. In fact, this calling is so sacred to the heart of God that it becomes much easier to recognize who has a true calling to be a prophet and who does not by how these types of words are delivered to people. Mature prophets of God will never deliver weighty and corrective words of prophecy without agony and at times with much weeping and prayer. A true prophet will continually find him/herself caught in the tension of standing before a holy God and yet called to minister to sinful man. Authentic prophets cringe at, but must embrace, their assignment at times to turn the people back to God through cries for repentance, holiness, and returning to first love.

Those in the body of Christ who have been given the gift of prophecy have limitations placed upon them per 1 Corinthians 14. The prophetic words they deliver must be full of encouragement, comfort, and strength. However, and as mentioned above, true prophets will not only follow the guidelines mentioned in 1 Corinthians 14 but they have also been given permission and capacity to confront, rebuke, expose, and uproot when necessary (see Jeremiah 1; Revelation 2, 3).

Will prophets continually and always move in this capacity? Absolutely not! In fact, if prophets only confront and rebuke and never build up and plant, they are unbalanced and dangerous. Prophets operate in a healthy prophetic anointing when they edify, exhort, and comfort, but they may also at times challenge and expose demonic practices, doctrinal error, and false prophets who endorse unbiblical standards not found in the Word of God.

Prophetic Jurisdiction

Why do prophets have this jurisdiction that saints with the gift of prophecy do not have? The answer is simple: The process and training that God puts true prophets through is entirely different because He has entrusted them with a weightier and deeper call upon their life. Many prophets go through severe trial and testing, not because of the sin in their life, but because of the prophetic call on their life. In order for cleansing and purification to come to the contemporary prophetic movement, true prophets themselves will have to be cleansed and purged. While saints may have a gift of prophecy, prophets themselves are the gift to the body of Christ.

Their calling is not only to deliver the message God has given them, but with time and maturity, they will become the message God has given them and it will carry a very high cost and involve much pain and suffering. Simply put, the price that true prophets will pay to operate in their calling versus those who have the spontaneous and occasional gift of prophecy is entirely and visibly different.

Wilderness Training

The primary difference between those who have been called as prophets of God and those who carry the gift of prophecy is found in whether or not they have been trained in the wilderness. The wilderness is the training ground for every true prophet of God. It destroys fleshly ambition. It wrecks the need to be seen. It teaches humility in ways that none of us can teach ourselves, destroying every fleshly confidence in self until nothing remains but a purified hunger for the Lord Himself.

> "The wilderness is the training ground for every true prophet of God."

It is in the wilderness where authentic prophets find their voice. They learn how to die to pride and arrogance and become dependent upon God for everything. Taking up the cross and following Jesus is center stage in the wilderness. The training and development of true prophets of God is so thorough and intense that anyone who actually desires to be a prophet is either ignorant of the wilderness seasons of preparation or simply believes they hold the office of prophet, but in truth they do not. True prophets of God walk with a limp. Most prophets don't even necessarily desire to be prophets. They understand the cost involved in their calling. Mature prophets have the scars to prove the authority they walk in as they have paid a steep price that few understand or will ever recognize.

The Tension Prophets Live In

Listen now to the agony that Jeremiah the prophet experienced as he penned these words to the Lord concerning his divine prophetic calling,

> *O Lord, You have deceived me and I was deceived; You have overcome me and prevailed...If I say, "I will not remember Him or speak anymore in His name," then in my heart it becomes like a burning fire...and I cannot endure it* (Jeremiah 20:7-9 NASB95).

The call on Jeremiah the prophet was so difficult that he began to say to God (paraphrased), "You tricked me! You deceived me! I can't get away from You. Every time I try and busy myself with other things, Your word becomes like a fire in my bones. God, I don't want to deliver these hard words. It's Your fault! You put me up to this."

Yes, true prophets carry weighty words full of revelation, correction, and direction, but this is a sacred trust they have been given by God Himself because of the difficult training they have endured. True prophets never enjoy or look forward to delivering correction and rebuke. Supposed "prophets" who release heavy-handed words without brokenness and the heart of the Father have clearly not been through the wilderness training that tested prophets go through.

If the contemporary prophetic movement is to be cleansed and purified, we must see the emergence of true prophets in the body of Christ who are received and embraced. Yes, they will build and, yes, they will plant, but they also fulfill their mandate by challenging, confronting, tearing down, and exposing. We cannot throw them away or dismiss these true prophets any longer just because they carry the capacity to disrupt and challenge accepted religious practices and traditions of men.

Prophets Need Apostles

Prophets have the tendency to wander around in circles because their eyes are so focused on the future. They desperately need apostles to help them to build and live for the present. Prophets constantly get caught chasing never-ending revelation and pursuing new spiritual experiences. They need apostles to hold their feet to the fire to study and actually know the Word of God. Prophets are prone to wander around and become lone rangers. They need apostles to father them, work alongside them, instruct them, and correct them.

Apostles help the prophets find their orientation and direction. Apostles will establish kingdom government in the lives of prophets and bring great emotional balance and stability to them. In many ways, apostles act as the anchor to the prophet's ministry (see Ephesians 2:20).

Apostles and prophets must learn how to function together as a team in this hour. Every apostle needs a prophet and every prophet needs an apostle (see 1 Corinthians 12:28). The prophets bring great confirmation and revelation to God's apostles and the apostles bring great emotional stability and balance to the prophets of God. Healthy prophets are always connected to fathering apostles and healthy apostles are always connected to revelatory prophets. We must learn how to work together and not compete against one another in the days we are living in.

> **"Apostles help the prophets find their orientation and direction."**

Prophets Are Not Lone Rangers

Prophets do not walk alone. They are only effective when they are in relationship with the body of Christ. In the New Testament, the prophet Agabus maintained credibility and integrity through his relationship to the church in Jerusalem and the apostles in general. Agabus was reputed to be a prophet, not because he called himself a prophet, but because his words consistently came to pass.

In Antioch there was a group of teachers and prophets who were tightly knit together (see Acts 13). When the council in Jerusalem made a ruling on behalf of the Gentile churches, they sent their decision in a letter through Paul and Barnabas. They also chose two prophets to accompany Paul and Barnabas. *"And Judas and Silas, being prophets also themselves, exhorted the brethren with many words, and confirmed them"* (Acts 15:32 KJV). Prophets were not lone rangers. They were submitted to the apostles and held in highest regard by the church community.

Paul wrote the following instructions for prophets in the local assembly: *"Let the prophets speak two or three, and let the other judge"* (1 Corinthians 14:29 KJV). Prophets operated in communion with other prophets. They flowed together yielding to one another. If anything is revealed to another who is sitting, let the first hold his peace (see 1 Corinthians 14:30). The prophets also judged and discerned the revelation as each spoke.

A prophet who refuses to subject his revelation to the body for judgment is destined to land in the ditch of error. He thinks that he is only in submission to Yahweh, and no one can question him. The prophets were in submission to one another: *"And the spirits of the prophets are subject to the prophets"* (1 Corinthians 14:32 KJV). When we read that

Agabus showed up prophesying, we must realize that his prophetic credibility and integrity were developed within the context of community. Prophets love to be with the body of Christ and fivefold ministers. Paul and Silas ministered together as an apostle and prophet team. Apostles and prophets especially love to be in the worship and prayer time. They love and honor the other ministry gifts.

Prophets Are Not Apostles

I had a prophetic dream in March of 2019 in which God spoke to me this phrase, "Beware of the prophets who think they are apostles."

Having never read or heard of this anywhere before, I inquired of the Lord in the dream and asked Him for more revelation and understanding into what He was saying and trying to reveal to me. He said, "Jeremiah, there are too many prophets in the earth who think they are apostles. They are attempting to function in a grace that I have not given them and they will become a great danger to My body if they continue in this error and are not corrected."

He went on, "There are some rare cases, as with Barnabas, where I called him as a prophet and eventually transitioned him into apostleship, but that was an extreme circumstance that should never be considered the standard."

I said, "Lord, what are some of the warning signs that will appear if those who are prophets are thinking and trying to act like apostles?"

He said, "First of all, they will be trying to operate in a grace that I have not granted them, and because of this, they will control and manipulate to get their agenda fulfilled. They will have a deep need to be validated by the title of an 'apostle' because that's where they believe their new identity should be found. They will slowly grow in pride, arrogance, and hunger for material possessions like never before.

"Most damaging of all," God said, "are these prophets who think they are apostles who have no revelation of sonship. They will counterfeit the true calling of reproducing sons and daughters (the work of an apostle) with multi-level marketing schemes and avoid the process of maturity that apostolic grace releases. They will claim to have sons and daughters when really they are just making disciples after themselves. They will falsely represent authentic apostolic ministry and must be corrected of this error before great destruction comes to My body."

One last time I inquired in the dream and asked, "Lord, but what about those extreme cases? How can we recognize if You are transitioning an individual called as a prophet to function as an apostle?"

He responded and said, "There will be three main things to look for if and when this transition happens. However, this process usually involves many years of training and equipping."

I immediately responded and said, "So Lord, are You saying that all these prophets who turn into apostles year after year are illegitimate?"

He said, "Absolutely. If they have endured the process and I have truly transitioned them, they will bear the three following marks."

1. *Increased Humility*

He said, "The transition from a prophet to authentic apostleship will involve a greater humbling than ever before. Humiliating circumstances and an invitation to true servanthood will be evident during this time period."

2. *More Crushing*

He said, "The transition into authentic apostleship brings more crushing than all of the other ministries. Truly those whom I have called who bear the marks of an apostle will have clearly picked up their cross and died to themselves. They will come through fire so hot that many of them will still be smoking when they stand before men."

> **"When a prophet claims to have become an apostle and no clear fathering and laying on of hands has taken place, it is a dangerous warning sign to all they come into contact with."**

3. More Fathering

He said, "Most evident of all in the transition from one called as a prophet to apostleship will be the impact of fathering and the correction that is needed for the days ahead. When a prophet claims to have become an apostle and no clear fathering and laying on of hands has taken place, it is a dangerous warning sign to all they come into contact with. From a prophet into authentic apostleship does not require days but years!" Then I woke up.

The Revelation of Home

One of the biggest problems in the fivefold ministry today is the number of apostolic and prophetic ministries who spend hardly any time in a home church. These itinerant ministers are away too many weeks in a year and lose the ability to have meaningful, accountable relationships with a particular body of people. While many of them claim to have national accountability, they lack weekly interaction with saints and local church leadership, which allows them the luxury of ministering to a corporate body on the weekends that they aren't really even a part of on a daily/weekly basis.

Too many apostolic and prophetic ministers tend to speak at another conference or church every weekend. I personally had to learn that this lifestyle and schedule greatly damages the revelation apostles and prophets receive and makes it impossible to develop and shepherd prophetic words to fruition and see order and kingdom authority established among the saints long term. In other words, these traveling apostles and prophets continually drop revelation seeds in everyone's pockets, but have rarely built anything for themselves or helped another labor to see a dream come forth.

I see a radical shift coming to many traveling apostolic and prophetic ministries. Many of them are going to grow very weary of bringing temporary change to church communities they hardly know on the weekend without ever investing in a community of believers they are in long-term love relationship with. Look in the epistles and document the numerous times the apostles stayed for months and even several years in one body until the work was accomplished or ready to be handed off.

We are about to witness many traveling apostles and prophets spend way less time on the road and way more time planting churches, pioneering for years, and working alongside other fivefold ministries for decades. Many of them every year are even going to take several months completely off from traveling to receive fresh revelation and strategy from the Lord.

Apostles, Prophets, and Intercessors

The kingdom of God is powerfully established and advanced when apostles, prophets, and intercessors each work together in the specific function/assignment that God has given them. When unified and operating with clarity, these three groups tear down demonic strongholds and plant and establish the kingdom of God in the earth. Let's look closely at how they partner together:

1. *The Prophets*

The prophets receive and release the words and heart of God through dreams, visions, and other means to apostles and intercessors. Prophets save and spare apostles and intercessors from *unnecessary labor and warfare!* Rather than intercessors trying to dig for revelation and insight, prophets give it to them with little to no time wasted. This allows intercessors to engage in informed prayer or *prophetic intercession*. Prophets also release the word of the Lord to apostles, which, oftentimes, simply confirms what the apostles are receiving in prayer and study of God's Word. Many apostles are waiting to put things into motion until they get a witness from a prophetic voice. They view it as permission and confirmation to move forward.

2. *The Apostles*

The apostles are called to *mobilize* and put into *motion* the word and heart of God. This is why it is so important that apostles are working in close relationship with the prophets. The prophet will see in part and the apostle will come and bring a *fullness* perspective to what the prophet has seen. Prophets carry the gift of vision but, oftentimes, lack the administrative gifting that apostles carry. Apostles call forth the intercessors and have them begin to mobilize the word of the Lord through strategic prayer assignments and covering of leaders and their families. True prophets are a blessing to apostles and help keep them from becoming rigid, legalistic, controlling, and authoritarian. Prophets are called to keep apostles from functioning from the position of the "letter that kills" and move them to the place of "the Spirit that gives life." Prophets must work closely together with apostles so that blind spots can be revealed.

3. *The Intercessors*

When intercessors are not connected to true apostles and prophets, they will grow tired, weary, and disillusioned. Many of them who are simply connected to shepherds (pastors) will at times become convinced that they are going crazy. Most intercessors are familiar with giving the word of the Lord to their pastor but have never really been led by apostles and prophets who give them the word of the Lord. Intercessors help advance the plans and purposes of God by standing in the gap and declaring the word of the Lord. They also help to mobilize and put into

> **"Intercessors help advance the plans and purposes of God by standing in the gap and declaring the word of the Lord."**

motion the promises of God by stirring up communities of believers to wake up and get involved.

I believe that the misunderstanding of how apostles, prophets, and intercessors are supposed to be working together has seriously hindered the establishing and advancing of the kingdom of God. At its core, *pride* is the greatest enemy of these three groups because, at times, they are all convinced that they are carrying the greatest revelation and strategy that no one else has. May God release a spirit of humility and purity that is necessary for these individuals to work together for the glory of God. Now is the time!

Apostles and Prophets Release Vision

The vision that apostles and prophets carry from the Spirit of God is directed toward the *universal* and *wider* body of Christ. This is in contrast to shepherds (pastors) and teachers who carry vision from the Holy Spirit that is generally directed toward a specific and local gathering of people.

Without the vision that apostles and prophets carry, local churches become self-focused, stagnant, and are constantly plagued by tunnel vision. These assemblies primarily become inwardly focused over time rather than empowered to advance the kingdom in their city and region.

> **"It takes a heart of humility to confess that we as church leaders need one another."**

If you are a pastor or teacher and do not acknowledge and invite the ministries of the apostles and prophets into your church community, the vision you have there is too small and must be expanded upon. You must invite the prophets (they see) and the apostles (they mobilize) to impart a greater vision and plan of action in your midst. It takes a heart of humility to confess that we as church leaders need one another. The fivefold ministry must learn how to work together in this hour!

Note

1. Brian Troxel, "Prophetic Purpose," August 1, 2017, https://aword.info/hear-his-prophets.

CHAPTER 6

APOSTOLIC WINESKINS

On Father's Day weekend of 2021, the Spirit of God visited me in an extraordinary way through a series of prophetic dreams in which I received several very detailed and lengthy night visions of what apostolic ministry can and will look like in the new era. My prayer is that what the Holy Spirit revealed to me concerning apostolic ministry in the decades ahead might bring confirmation, enlightenment, and encouragement to many. May Jesus Christ be glorified!

The Five Apostolic Highlights

In the series of prophetic dreams, I was escorted by the Holy Spirit to cities all over the world. He made it very clear to me that what He is highlighting in apostolic ministry is not bound to a geographic location. I specifically remember visiting Dallas, Texas, New York City, the United Kingdom, Australia, Russia, China, and many other nations. In every place we visited, I saw the phrase *apostolic hubs* on sign-posts wherever I looked. The Holy Spirit took issue time and time again with the religious use of the word *church*, which I understood in the dream had greatly grieved Him. From His perspective, *apostolic hub* was much more of a necessary and accurate description of what was taking place *and* allowed Him to move more freely rather than labeling the gathering of people as a "church" in the traditional use of the word.

As we traveled around to these "apostolic hubs" in the earth, the Holy Spirit began to highlight five specific aspects of apostolic ministry that He is breathing on now and in the years ahead. They are:

1. Apostles and Team Ministry
2. Apostles and Deliverance
3. Apostles and Prayer
4. Apostles and the Crucified Christ
5. Apostles and the Fatherhood of God

Apostles and Team Ministry

God began to show me His desire to join apostles and prophets together around the globe. I specifically saw apostles with blueprints from above who are lacking the breath of God upon what they are doing, because they are not actively laboring with prophets who are called to prophesy the word of the Lord to them. Prophets are called to be a blessing to apostles and keep them from becoming too rigid, legalistic, and authoritarian regarding wineskins.

I saw apostles gathering companies of young apostles and discipling them in the ways and mysteries of Christ. A divine exchange among generations will take place that will release authentic power and authority.

I saw a massive geographic shift take place in the earth where a number of apostles who have labored alone or have been misunderstood for years are going to transition to a new field (location) where they will labor alongside other five-fold ministers. As they move into these territories and come alongside other established works, these "churches" will look less and less traditional and more New Testament in DNA and expression in the years ahead.

Apostles and Deliverance

The Holy Spirit said to me that He is raising up apostles in the earth who are going to specialize and emphasize the casting out of devils. He showed me His grief regarding this lack of what He said was "an absolutely necessary kingdom of God expression."

I saw an unusual fire and zeal overtake many apostles in the years ahead. This passion will cause apostles of deliverance to team up and hold outdoor gatherings in tents, stadiums, parks, and even in the streets to demonstrate the power of God.

I was also allowed to peer into the cloud of witnesses and saw Lester Sumrall and Derek Prince. They had specific prayer assignments to apostles of deliverance that they might teach and instruct with sound doctrine and true holy living.

I finally saw a mocking, religious spirit assigned to attack apostles of deliverance. This thorn in the flesh is a harassing spirit from Christians who need deliverance themselves. A spirit of humility and love is the key to defeating this spirit's grip.

Apostles and Prayer

The Holy Spirit began to show me a realm of legislation through intercession in the years ahead that will have crippling effects on demonic strongholds and regional principalities. Look for the apostles of deliverance and apostles of prayer to partner together to release simultaneous mass deliverance and a serious spirit of travail upon the saints.

> **"Messages and songs in tongues will break out in corporate gatherings on an unprecedented level."**

The Holy Spirit shared with me His desire to release spiritual language all across the earth that has never been heard before. There will be a tremendous increase of the baptism of the Holy Spirit with evidence of tongues in the years ahead. Messages and songs in tongues will break out in corporate gatherings on an unprecedented level. Astounding salvations will take place as individuals hear their own language from strangers of a different ethnicity.

I saw "schools of prayer" emerge all over the earth. Literal discipling of people into a lifestyle of prayer and fasting will be a hallmark of many apostles of prayer in the days ahead.

The power and anointing of Pentecost is going to rest on several apostles of prayer in the next several decades. These men and women are going to be distributors of the glory of God. They have specifically been assigned to denominations and will be holy wrecking balls to the status quo.

Apostles and the Crucified Christ

The Holy Spirit showed me a tremendous shift in apostolic ministry in the years ahead that will involve house to house gatherings that will recapture the organic nature of the New Testament Church. These apostles have absolutely no interest in trying to reform the existing structure of church in their city and region.

The Holy Spirit also showed me many apostles who are currently referred to as "pastor" of their church who have allowed themselves to wear a religious garment that they can no longer wear. In the years ahead, many apostles are going to totally shift the infrastructure of their churches to take the focus and dependence off of themselves and truly equip saints for the work of the ministry. Look for them to shift everything from service schedules to what days of the week they are going to meet.

I saw a tremendous emphasis in apostolic ministry in the years ahead on the crucified life of Christ and embracing His humanity before ever walking in divinity. Entire communities of believers across the globe are going to be established on the cross of Christ, and many will find true joy there that they could never find for years attending traditional church.

Fathering, mothering, and family are going to be a key emphasis in these gatherings.

Apostles and the Fatherhood of God

I was made aware by the Holy Spirit how deeply grieved He is concerning the religious theatrics and performance in much of what we call the church today. I saw thousands and thousands of individuals who had attended church their whole life who, from heaven's perspective, were religious orphans.

I saw apostles of the fatherhood of God emerging all over the earth who will encourage, comfort, and speak to the wounds that religion has brought to many generations. They will minister on sonship and adoption with such clarity and potency that it will dismantle the fear and religious control that many Christians have known their entire life.

Where these apostles of the fatherhood of God minister, they will reproduce after their own kind. An entire new breed of Christian will be born and reborn in the earth in the new era that will never know what religious fear, manipulation, and orphanhood is all about. This promise will be what will keep these apostles encouraged over the years so they do not forget their labor of love is not in vain.

I have journaled and stewarded this visitation from the Holy Spirit concerning apostolic ministry on Father's Day weekend to the best of my abilities. I remind us that all prophecy must be tested and judged (see 1 Corinthians 14:29). I therefore openly invite leaders and saints in the body of Christ to weigh this visitation against the written Word of God and His character and nature. My intent in publishing this encounter is not that it would become an authority on apostolic ministry but rather serve as a blueprint and prayer agenda for us all in the new era.

CHAPTER 7

PROPHETIC REFORMATION

We live in critical days for the global prophetic movement.

The need for purity, humility, and transparency has never been greater. A generation of prophetic messengers is emerging who carries a specific assignment to confront the body of Christ with their boredom of God. These burning and shining lamps will cry out to the Church like Jeremiah of old and declare, *"What injustice did your fathers find in Me, that they went far from Me, and walked after emptiness and became empty?"* (Jeremiah 2:5 NASB). These prophetic voices of reformation will be filled with the knowledge of God and restore awe and wonder to the Bride once again.

The Prophetic Showdown

I have spent the last several months combing through the Old Testament prophets and the ministry of Jesus Christ, who I recognize as the greatest New Testament prophet. My renewed study and fresh research has led me to believe that if a prophet is true to their specific calling and grace given by God, they will feel deeply and speak loudly into five primary national issues concerning:

- The Shedding of Innocent Blood
- Sexual Immorality and Wickedness
- The Treatment of the Poor and Needy
- The Spiritual State of Nations and the Church
- Salvation in Jesus Christ and His Second Coming

It is these five primary arenas that I believe modern-day prophets are called and graced to speak into. Our great challenge in the 21st century is that many who we call "prophets" have refused to speak into many of these arenas and instead have become spiritual psychics and fortune tellers. For example, instead of prophets raising up their voice concerning abortion and sexual immorality, they stay silent to keep their following and cover their own compromise.

Instead of taking up the cause of the poor and challenging the Church concerning her love of money, too many so-called modern-day prophets refuse to speak up because they know it will cost them the platforms they have built for themselves. Rather than call the Church to consecration, repentance, and to prepare for the Second Coming of Christ, "prophets" are strengthening people in their sin by telling them God is at peace with them when He, in fact, is not.

It is for these errors and reasons that I believe we are heading for a prophetic showdown between the true and false prophets around the world. When national and global decisions are made concerning abortion and sexual immorality, it will be easy to see which prophets serve Baal and those who do not by how they choose to cry aloud or remain silent.

We must have a prophetic reformation in this new era where we constantly stay alert in the place of prayer and consume the Word of God. The eyes of the spiritually blind are going to be opened in the decades ahead.

The Current Crisis

In many circles in which I currently travel around the world, unfortunately, prophetic ministry has become not only a laughing matter among church leaders, but is considered unreliable and inaccurate by a growing number of disillusioned saints. We are witnessing one prophetic word after another fall to the ground from well-known prophetic voices, and no one is held accountable or even offers to repent for their mistakes. In other circles, prophetic ministry has become so politically correct that any prophetic words of warning, rebuke, and correction are categorically rejected.

God's Answer

I believe that God's answer to the crisis currently facing the prophetic movement is the "Micaiah Company." These are prophetic voices who will not go with the status quo. Many of them, right now, are engaged in a battle for their destiny. In 1 Kings 22, Micaiah initially echoed what the other prophets of his day were saying, but when pressed by the hand of God, he knew that he had to deliver the word of the Lord, regardless of whom it offended and what kind of platform he would lose.

I believe there are many Micaiahs all over the earth, still undecided as to where their allegiance lies. Will they echo along with their contemporaries what the people want to hear, or will they walk in the fear of the Lord and deliver to the people what they need to hear? Make no mistake, the path of the Micaiah Company is a road less traveled, full of rejection and loneliness at times, yet it's a path of glory filled with the affirmation and applause of the Father. It's time for the Micaiahs in the earth to come out of hiding and get off the fence. These are the days when you will finally recognize why you were created. You indeed were born for such a time as this!

> **"It's time for the Micaiahs in the earth to come out of hiding and get off the fence."**

I see a growing trend in the contemporary prophetic culture in which everything must be positive, politically correct, and performance based or it can't be from God. It is a trend toward releasing and embracing only general encouragement and words full of false hope that often have too little substance or depth. These words sound good in the moment but carry little weight long term. This shift and crisis in the current contemporary prophetic movement mirrors the shift and crisis that Jeremiah experienced in Bible times. He cried out in agony and prophesied to his peers, saying, "You are addressing the wounds of the people superficially. You are crying out, 'Peace, peace' when there is no peace" (see Jeremiah 6:14).

As in the days of Jeremiah, so too the current contemporary prophetic culture in America largely rejects or ignores calls to repentance, cries for reform, and confrontations of specific sin in the land. Jeremiah went even further to address how the general public would respond to prophetic words that are positive, politically correct, and performance based, *"The prophets prophesy falsely, and the priests rule on their own authority; **and My people love it so!** But what will you do at the end of it?"* (Jeremiah 5:31 NASB95). Just as the people in Jeremiah's day loved false prophecies of hope and peace, so too many in the 21st century have joined this same chorus.

Nevertheless, God has mercifully raised up voices in every generation that have confronted trending prophetic patterns. These voices are themselves prophets, but they have been called by God to resist and expose the false and immature prophets in the land.

God raised up Leonard Ravenhill in his generation to cry out with great clarity regarding prophetic ministry. He said:

> The prophet comes to set up that which is upset. His work is to call into line those who are out of line! He is unpopular because he opposes the popular in morality and spirituality. In a day of faceless politicians and voiceless preachers, there is not a more urgent national need than our cry to God for a prophet![1]

Spontaneous Prophecy

Two types of prophecy exist: spontaneous prophecy and revelatory prophecy. All believers are capable of prophesying on a spontaneous level, particularly in small group settings and even in worship. Paul addresses this gift in 1 Corinthians 14:1-5. The saints can bring edification, exhortation, and comfort to the body of Christ on many levels. Spontaneous prophecy rarely offends people (it shouldn't), and it finds its roots in encouragement and blessing. Spontaneous prophecy can be given by individuals who are not prophets of the Lord, but who are simply exercising the momentary gift of prophecy. On the other hand, revelatory prophecy can be given only by prophets themselves. While prophets can operate in both spontaneous and revelatory prophecy, ordinary believers who operate in the gift of prophecy are limited to spontaneous prophecy.

Contemporary prophetic culture wholeheartedly embraces spontaneous prophecy. They love and enjoy the general blessing and encouragement that comes through believers who move in the gift of prophecy as well as through prophets themselves. The crisis comes when the only form of acceptable prophecy in the land is spontaneous prophecy. What about revelatory prophecy? Could it be that in labeling believers who operate in spontaneous prophecy as "prophets," we are actually misleading and bringing confusion to a subject that really needs clarity and direction?

Revelatory Prophecy

Spontaneous prophecy is a valid and intricate part of church life, but revelatory prophecy goes much deeper. Revelatory prophecy is born in the place of prayer and fasting. It then requires days, weeks, and even months of careful prayer and meditation before it is released. Revelatory prophecy by nature is simply too directive, too corrective, and too predictive to be delivered on a whim. If you asked a prophetic voice when was the last time that they went on an extended fast before releasing the "word of the Lord," what would they say? If you asked them when was the last time they didn't just receive a "word" and then immediately shotgun it out on social media, what would they say? Would it be too extreme to say that there is more spontaneous prophecy being released to the body of Christ than revelatory prophecy?

Revelatory prophecy often calls for repentance and warns of the consequences if the word of the Lord is ignored. Words of warning are the Lord's last real attempt to keep us on track or restore us to the right path. Prophets cannot give revelatory words with the same freedom as they do spontaneous words.

> "Revelatory prophecy is born in the place of prayer and fasting."

I believe God is positioning the bride of Christ in this hour to receive His discipline and rebuke and therefore His justice without interpreting it as rejection. His correction upon our lives is a demonstration of His goodness toward us as His people. The issue is not whether or not He loves us, but whether or not our own orphan hearts can receive His love for us. At times the words of the Father bring great comfort to our hearts, and in other seasons His words sting in order to bring adjustment. We must always remember that whether the words comfort or sting, they still come from the same voice of our loving Father.

Let me be clear! While I do not believe that correction and discipline (judgment) are the primary ways God deals with us as His children under the New Covenant, to throw out these aspects of His character and nature altogether and say that the cross of Jesus Christ did away with them is not founded upon the full counsel of God. As prophetic people, we must take careful consideration and observation of *all Scripture* before we make blanket statements. God is a good and gracious Father, but in His truth and just nature He will bring about correction and discipline for our good. As Hebrews 12:6

> **"We must always remember that whether the words comfort or sting, they still come from the same voice of our loving Father."**

(NASB95) says, *"For those whom the Lord loves He disciplines, and He scourges every son whom He receives."*

When God's Warnings Aren't Positive Enough

Several years ago I was ministering to a group of leaders and students who had gone through supernatural and prophetic training from a very popular Christian movement. While I was preaching, I had a strange spiritual experience in which I was shown an assignment from the devil against a particular leader and his wife. I outlined three specific attacks that their marriage would face over the next seven years and assured them of victory as God gave them clear direction of hope in the midst of trial through the prophetic word. I have never felt the love of God for a particular couple like I did that night.

After the meeting, the couple in leadership whom I had prophesied over came up to me and said that they renounced everything I said to them because it wasn't positive enough. They said their prophetic and supernatural training had instructed them to not receive any negative words.

Sadly, this couple was divorced within that same year. Isn't it amazing that I was personally encountering the love of God for that couple as I prophesied to them because He was so kind to warn and expose them to the devil's plans ahead of time, yet they failed to receive it because it wasn't "positive" enough?

And trust me, that situation I encountered years ago has been repeated over and over again. Much of the current contemporary prophetic movement is teaching saints to not receive God's warnings and referring to them as "curses," from "the devil," "Old Testament-like," and so on.

Can you imagine Noah telling God that the message about the flood wasn't positive enough? Can you imagine Joseph telling God that the dream about the slaughter of infants wasn't positive enough? Can you imagine Agabus telling God that the coming famine wasn't positive enough? How about the five out of seven churches in the book of Revelation who were rebuked and corrected by Jesus Christ Himself?

My prayer for the global body of Christ is that we will simply receive what God has to say, no matter how severe or

gentle it is. Why do we continue to create immature prophetic saints who are continually blindsided by the enemy?
People are "binding" God's warnings and calling them curses
or too negative because they don't really know Him. I have
learned how to rejoice when God warns me through His
prophets. When the words of warning, correction, and
rebuke come, I rejoice! I thank God for His love and kindness for my life. He cares
enough that if I'm head-
ing down the wrong
path, He will fire warn-
ing shots time and
time again.

As prophets and
prophetic people, if
we believe that God as
Father is incapable of
disciplining His kids,

> **"Nowhere in Scripture does God promise peace, prosperity, and blessing to individuals, ministries, and nations who walk according to the counsel of the wicked."**

every prophetic word we release, regardless of how a person
responds to the truth of God in their lives, will assure them
that only blessing and hope are around the corner. Nowhere
in Scripture does God promise peace, prosperity, and blessing
to individuals, ministries, and nations who walk according to
the counsel of the wicked.

In other prophetic circles, such an emphasis is placed
on the judgment and correction of God that any word that
remotely speaks of God's desire as Father to bring healing and

restoration to His people is categorically rejected. Prophetic words filled with destiny, hope, and the promise of revival are thrown out the window because God is now fed up with the sin of the people. As prophetic voices, if we believe that God the Father is incapable of demonstrating His kindness and goodness to His people, every prophetic word that we release, regardless of how a person responds to the truth of God in their lives, will carry an unnecessary corrective and judgmental tone.

The Micaiah Company

The Micaiah Company rising in the earth will not only know God the Father as a good and kind God, but also as God and Father who disciplines because He loves. Whether it's a word of rebuke and correction or a word of affirmation and applause, they will not reject certain aspects of God's character and nature while accepting others. They will not be limited by their personal experience and will take into consideration the full counsel of God as they sit before Him.

As prophetic people, we must ask ourselves, "What aspects of God's character and nature do I currently understand, and therefore am capable of releasing to His people, and what aspects of His character and nature quite frankly make me uncomfortable, and therefore limit me in my ability to minister to His people? Have I had hurtful experiences in the past that prevent me from receiving all of who God is?" The Micaiah Company is not only capable of prophesying incredible words of hope, destiny, and healing, but they are also trained in releasing words of correction, rebuke, and calls for repentance.

Maturing in the Prophetic

I want to try to articulate as clearly as I can that to continue majoring on certain aspects of God's character and nature and to minor on, or plainly ignore, others is both unhealthy and leaves the prophetic movement greatly limited and ineffective in its impact on the body of Christ. Some prophetic people have an exceedingly great revelation of the kindness and graciousness of God, while others possess an immeasurable grace to deliver words full of correction and rebuke.

We must be very careful not to emphasize and magnify certain aspects of who God is to the degree that the people of God become totally unfamiliar and uncomfortable with other aspects. Whether God's goodness and kindness make us uneasy or His ability to correct and bring adjustment makes us cringe, we must give ourselves to allowing God the Father to work into us the aspects of His character and nature that we do not yet possess. A fully mature prophet will carry and embrace every aspect of the character and nature of God and be graced with the ability to deliver at any moment to any individual the portion of who God is that the person is in need of.

We must see prophetic ministry as God inviting His people through His servants into a full-on participation and encounter with His character and nature, rather than being spectators of the words He releases. I see prophetic schools in the days ahead spending way more time teaching prophetic people about the character and nature of God, and much less time on the mechanics of prophecy. Our desires in the prophetic movement to get words of knowledge for people and various details of their lives to produce a "wow factor" have too often derailed God's desire to impart His character and nature to His people. How are people's lives really transformed into the character of Christ when they leave prophetic meetings talking more about the prophet than the God of the prophet?

> **"How are people's lives really transformed into the character of Christ when they leave prophetic meetings talking more about the prophet than the God of the prophet?"**

Once again, one of the primary roles of a prophetic voice is to assist people in their ultimate calling in life, which is to be conformed into the image of Jesus Christ, the Son (see Romans 8:29). In essence, we have too many prophetic voices ready to tell people what God wants to do for them and not enough messengers ready to tell people who God wants to be for them.

Delivering Corrective Words of Prophecy

While I believe that delivering words of discipline from the Father is reserved for New Testament prophets and not for those who operate in an occasional gift of prophecy, I also believe that corrective words of prophecy should never be delivered spontaneously in a public gathering. I have rarely seen a corrective word of prophecy that was delivered in this manner bear fruit, not only because it was released in the wrong setting, but because it was so vague that it created more confusion than clarity.

As a believer who operates in the gift of prophecy, if all you ever receive and deliver are words of correction and rebuke for people, you need to go back and read 1 Corinthians 14 and, while you're at it, cry out for a revelation of the character and nature of God. And if you are called to be a New Testament prophet and all you ever release are hard and judgmental words toward leaders and the body of Christ, you must pursue and embrace every aspect of God's character and nature so that those who sit under your ministry might receive a mature and complete revelation of who God is!

Church leadership should not have to worry about some bizarre prophet walking into the back of the church building (and of course no one has ever seen them before) to issue a rebuke to the leadership for hidden sin or a number of different issues. This is completely out of alignment with the heart of the Father for the New Testament Church. A prophet's behavior should put a ministry team at ease, rather than on the edge of their seats with unnecessary fear. The Micaiah Company have been sent to local assemblies to be blessings rather than create collateral damage!

With all of this being said, I absolutely believe that there is a place for corrective prophecy regarding the discipline of the Lord under the New Covenant, but it must never be given spontaneously and must be delivered only by broken and tested prophets. The issue at stake here for the Micaiah Company is how to effectively steward corrective words from the Father in a way that will bring forth the greatest amount of fruit. Standing up in the back of a church building unannounced and starting to shout or grabbing a microphone and screaming will not have a far-reaching impact upon the saints. Ultimately, it will be destructive rather than edifying to an assembly of believers, which again is not the heart of the Father for the New Testament Church.

Protocol and strategy must be established in a local assembly by church leadership to provide a place for tested and broken prophets to submit corrective words of prophecy. I believe that how we deliver a word must be seen as a key ingredient in the delivery and effect of it. The Micaiah Company are broken vessels that the Father can entrust with strong corrective words for individuals, ministries, and nations, because this is an aspect of His character and nature that He chooses to share with His people. This, as Hebrews 12:10 (NIV) says, is *"for our good, in order that we may share in his holiness."*

I believe with all my heart that an aspect of God's character and nature as revealed in the New Testament is His ability to train, adjust, correct and rebuke. But we must be very careful as the Micaiah Company that we are spending significant time with Him in prayer and fasting to allow Him to work His heart inside of us before we deliver His words. It is not enough to deliver His words. We must deliver them with His heart!

The abuse and misuse of this particular aspect of God's character and nature has done tremendous damage to the body of Christ and the prophetic movement itself. On the other hand, we are also witnessing an overemphasis on God's goodness and kindness at the expense of emphasizing

> **"It is not enough to deliver His words. We must deliver them with His heart!"**

His ability to discipline and bring correction to His body. This happens, in part, because so many prophets who have gone before us have prophesied out of their flesh and not from spending time standing in the counsel of the Lord to allow His character and nature to be fully formed inside of them.

I believe that in order for the prophetic movement to put childish ways behind them and truly grow up in this hour, we are going to have to stop allowing the extremes of our past experiences to dictate our present and future beliefs concerning who God is and how we are to minister His character and nature to His people. Just because the prophets of the past may have prophesied about a God who was angry, when really He was full of delight, does not mean we should currently prophesy about a God who is pleased when really He is upset, or vice versa. As the Micaiah Company, we must set aside extremes and even our own experiences and go on a journey to discover His character and nature as revealed in His Scripture. It is only through spending time with Him that we will carry an accurate revelation and interpretation of who He is and release it to the saints.

We desperately need clarity and revelation in the contemporary prophetic movement if we are going to navigate through the current crisis. We must begin to embrace and receive the Micaiah Company who move in revelatory prophecy and carry words that will shake cities, regions, and nations. As previously stated, I believe the way in which we choose to release this revelatory prophecy, especially in the local assembly, will have a large impact on the fulfillment of it.

Bring on the spontaneous and general encouragement! I love it! We need more of it! But oh, how we need the word of the Lord that corrects, instructs, chastises, warns, rebukes, and releases the fear of the Lord. Let's embrace the gift of prophecy that any believer can move in that seeks to edify, exhort, and bring consolation; but let's also embrace the ministry of the prophet found in Jeremiah 1:10 and Revelation 2 and 3 that rebukes, confronts, and warns. This is the counterbalance and reformation that the contemporary prophetic movement so desperately needs. If we will position ourselves in the global Church to receive both spontaneous and revelatory prophecy and seek to welcome the Micaiah Company in our midst, I believe there is hope for prophetic reformation in the new era.

Notes

1. Leonard Ravenhill, "Picture of a Prophet," 1994, http://www.ravenhill.org/prophet.htm.

CHAPTER 8

PASTORS, TEACHERS, AND EVANGELISTS

Ilove the local church. As a pastor's son of many years, my daycare was the church sanctuary where my siblings and I built the best forts with church chairs that you have ever seen, while my mother answered the phones as the church secretary. As teenagers, we shoveled the snow in the winter so the congregants could get in safely, and we cut the grass in the summer and ran through the fields. The memories I have are irreplaccable and have had a profound impact on my life.

As someone who went to college and earned a bachelor's degree in ministry that cost me eighty thousand dollars, I often tell people that what I learned as a pastor's son was more valuable, practical, and tangible than anything I ever learned in a classroom at a Christian university. All my life, I have never walked into a church building anywhere in the world and not smiled. I've never met a pastor and their family and not understood what it's really like behind the scenes. I thank God for the shepherds of God's flock. I honor the teachers of God's Word. I have greatly benefitted from evangelists who have preached the pure gospel and sought to fulfill the Great Commission.

I have spent quite a bit of time in the last few chapters writing about the role and function of apostles and prophets. Again, they are foundation layers who are graced to work together and pioneer in the establishing of the house of God. Those two ministries are desperately needed in the global church to reveal, demonstrate, and manifest the apostolic and prophetic side of Christ Jesus to His body. They are not better than the other three ministries. They simply come first and second in 1 Corinthians 12:28 because of the grace they have been given.

Pastors, teachers, and evangelists have been given *building ministries,* which means the work they are graced for in the house of God comes after apostles and prophets. All five ministries are necessary for the maturing of the body. Too many apostles and prophets reject the ministries of pastors, teachers, and evangelists because they do not understand their role and function. Apostles and prophets are geared more toward the raising up of the saints as an army to invade regions and territories. Apostles and prophets typically emphasize subjects such as the kingdom of God, revival, deliverance, spiritual authority, and so on. Pastors and teachers are focused more on caring for the sheep who are wounded, hurting, broken, and in need of discipleship. Pastors and teachers are often program driven while apostles and prophets are more presence driven. Both are needed! The focus of pastors and teachers is local. The focus of apostles and prophets is ultimately citywide and regional. Pastors and teachers view the church as a hospital for sinners. Apostles and prophets view the church as a military base for saints. Evangelists are graced as stone collectors outside of the house of God who win souls and bring them back to the house, which is made up of spiritual stones who are being built and fitted together into an eternal dwelling place of the Holy Spirit (see 1 Peter 2:5).

Each one of the five ministries is called to reveal, demonstrate, and manifest a certain aspect of who Jesus is. For example, modern day apostles are called to represent the apostolic nature of Jesus to His body and equip an apostolic people for the work of the ministry. Pastors are called to represent the shepherding nature of Jesus to His body and equip a pastoral people. The challenge in the body of Christ unfortunately is that we just want to fight about the specific aspect of Jesus that we like best or prefer. Evangelists shout about the need to win souls and fulfill the Great Commission, while the pastors are heartbroken over the condition of the flock. Prophets want revival and the manifestations of the Spirit, while teachers want more Bible studies and sound doctrine. I have learned over the years that each fivefold ministry even has their own set of Bible verses that they like to quote to justify their view and convictions. If we do not understand the grace on each ministry and our urgent need for every single one of them—because it's really all about Jesus Christ—we become a body who is tossed back and forth by every wind of doctrine, failing to mature and be established as a spiritual house (see Ephesians 4:21-22).

The Function of Pastors

Pastors are graced to counsel, marry, bury, care for, nourish, and encourage the body of Christ. Matthew 9:36 (NASB) says, *"Seeing the crowds, He felt compassion for them, because they were distressed and downcast, like sheep without a shepherd."* Jesus was the greatest pastor who ever lived. He revealed the essence of a pastoral heart when he said in Matthew 18:12 (NASB), *"If any man has a hundred sheep, and one of them goes astray, will he not leave the ninety-nine on the mountains, and go and search for the one that is lost?"* The hearts of true pastors are deeply concerned with the brokenness of humanity and how to care for their souls, marriages, and families. Pastors look for green grass and fresh water for the sheep. They bring peace, comfort, and assurance through life's greatest trials and tribulations. Pastors impart compassion, tenderness, and personal care for the people of God—especially the other four ministries. Without pastors,

> **"True pastoring cannot be done from behind a pulpit."**

apostles and prophets can lack the heart of God and fail to realize the way God cares for even their own souls.

It is worthy to note that true pastoring cannot be done from behind a pulpit. Pastors are highly relational individuals and the grace on their lives thrives in one on one and small group settings. They crave interacting with saints and the other four ministries on a deep heart and emotional level. They love transparency, vulnerability, hospitality, and love to invest in marriages and families.

The Teachers Among Us

It says that in Acts 13 at Antioch there were prophets and teachers among them. The disciples called Jesus "Rabbi" many times throughout the Gospels because they recognized this extraordinary gift He possessed (see John 1:38). Teachers have been graced by God to align the Church with His Word. When someone is called to be a fivefold teacher, they do more than give information—they carry an anointing to create a love for biblical truth in the body of Christ. Teachers help us to stay rooted and grounded in discipleship and sound doctrine. They are geared toward the line upon line, precept upon precept of Scripture. They are third in 1 Corinthians 12:28 because they have an extremely important role to play once the foundation has been laid and pioneering has been completed. They often challenge apostles and prophets on what they view as "extra biblical revelation." They will hear someone give a dream, vision, or prophetic exhortation and often ask, "Where is that in the Bible?" While they have a vital role and function to play, they also have to be careful that they are being led by the Holy Spirit in their convictions. Fivefold teachers can easily fall prey to a religious spirit, which causes them to become so focused on the scriptural minutia of issues they perceive wrong in the body that they miss the big picture of what God is saying and doing. Jesus called this straining out a gnat but swallowing a camel (see Matthew 23:24).

A Warning Dream

Several years ago I had a dream in which I saw all five ministries on a white board and God said to me, "Jeremiah, there is a specific cancer that seeks to cripple each of the five ministries." On the board was written:

- Apostles—Pride
- Prophets—Rejection
- Teachers—Legalism
- Pastors—Discouragement
- Evangelists—Vanity

Each ministry must overcome this specific cancer that is assigned to them to keep them from maturity and walking in the fullness of their calling.

The Centrality of God's Word

Pastors and teachers working together help the body of Christ in their great need to be cared for and build their lives upon the Word of God. Again, pastors have been graced to care for and nurture the people of God and teachers have been graced to make sure the body is feeding upon the Word of God. Second John 9 says (NASB), *"Anyone who goes too far and does not remain in the teaching of Christ, does not have God; the one who remains in the teaching has both the Father and the Son."* First Timothy 4:16 (NASB) also exhorts us, saying, *"Pay close attention to yourself and to the teaching; persevere in these things, for as you do this you will save both yourself and those who hear you."*

Where pastors and teachers are functioning together, they help the body of Christ recognize and embrace three main realities.

1. *The Church is a culture of truth, not a culture of feelings.*

Timothy understood the dangers of building based off of our feelings and not the truth when he wrote and described the church: *"the household of God, which is the church of the living God, the pillar and support of the truth"* (1 Timothy 3:15 NASB).

John Piper describes his thoughts so eloquently on the challenge this generation is having concerning our feelings and the truth when he writes and says:

> My feelings are not God. God is God. My feelings do not define truth. God's Word defines truth. My feelings are echoes and responses to

what my mind perceives. And sometimes, many times, my feeling are out of sync with the truth. When that happens, and it happens every day in some measure, I try not to bend the truth to justify my imperfect feelings, but rather, I plead with God: Purify my perceptions of your truth and transform my feelings so that they are in sync with the truth.[1]

It's important that saints understand that the way Jesus' words make us feel emotionally is not a good gauge of truth (see Matthew 19:22-25). When we hear the Word of God taught and preached, our first question should be "Is this true?" not "How did it make me feel?"

2. *You cannot separate Jesus from what He says and still have the real Jesus.*

Many in this generation are falling in love with a God of their imagination and not the God of the Bible. They enjoy separating the person of Jesus from the words of Jesus, and this is error. Mark 8:38 (NASB) says, *"For whoever is ashamed of Me and My words...the Son of Man will also be ashamed of him."* Again in John 12:48 (NASB95) Jesus says, *"He who rejects Me **and does not receive My sayings,** has one who judges him; the word I spoke is what will judge him at the last day."* In Luke 6:46 (NASB) Jesus makes it plain concerning this issue when He asks, *"Why do you call Me, 'Lord, Lord,' and do not do what I say?"*

3. *At the heart of discipleship is having our lives formed by God's Word.*

In John 8:30-47, we clearly see that the crowds had a lot of admiration and even affection for Jesus. They "believed in Him" as the Messiah, but they were not prepared to yield to the requirements of true faith and to be changed to the core by His words. How we relate to Jesus' words determines whether we are His disciples or not. Jesus' words cut across our own desires, ideas, and lifestyles. The test of discipleship is whether we will bow to His truth or hold on to our own thoughts and feelings. Jesus never sacrificed truth for winsomeness. Seven times Jesus mentioned "truth" in John 8:30-47. When winsomeness becomes our highest priority, then the truth always get thrown under the bus.

> **"How much will it take for you to sell the truth?"**

God and the devil are both asking the global Church the same questions today: How much will it take for you to sell the truth? The approval of culture? Tax-exempt status? Persecution? Proverbs 23:23 (NIV) says, *"Buy the truth and do not sell it."*

The Call to Discipleship

Pastors and teachers help the body of Christ get discipled. They care for their souls and teach them how to love the truth and not be deceived by their feelings. Disciples of Jesus Christ relate to His words in seven specific ways. Barry Nichols describes them in the following ways.

1. We bow to His words as our supreme authority.

> *"For My hand made all these things, so all these things came into being," declares the Lord. "But I will look to this one, at one who is humble and contrite in spirit, and who trembles at My word"* (Isaiah 66:2 NASB).

> *My flesh trembles in fear of you; I stand in awe of your laws* (Psalm 119:120 NIV).

2. We are honest with what He says, laying down our own desires and agenda.

Luke 8:15 (NASB) reminds us that a good and honest heart bears much fruit.

> *But the seed in the good soil, these are the ones who have heard the word with a good and virtuous heart, and hold it firmly, and produce fruit with perseverance.*

3. We treasure and embrace all of His words, not just those we find pleasing.

> *Therefore I esteem right all Your precepts concerning everything, I hate every false way* (Psalm 119:128 NASB95).

"If you believe what you like in the Gospel, and reject what you don't like, it is not the Gospel you believe, but yourself." —St. Augustine

4. We keep searching out His words, never resting only on what we already know or what others have said.

In Acts 17:11-12 (NASB), the Bereans were nobler because they searched the Scriptures to see if what Paul was saying was true.

Now these people were more noble-minded than those in Thessalonica, for they received the word with great eagerness, examining the Scriptures daily to see whether these things were so. Therefore, many of them believed, along with a significant number of prominent Greek women and men.

5. We have a heart bent on obeying what He says.

So I will keep Your Law continually, forever and ever. ...This has become mine, that I comply with Your precepts. ...I hurried and did not delay to keep Your commandments. ...I have inclined my heart to perform Your statutes forever, even to the end (Psalm 119:44, 56, 60, 112 NASB).

6. We keep holding to His words even when we don't understand, and we refuse to let go even when we are suffering.

> *I cling to Your testimonies; Lord, do not put me to shame! ...The arrogant utterly deride me, yet I do not turn aside from Your Law. ...The snares of the wicked have surrounded me, but I have not forgotten Your Law. ...Though I have become like a wineskin in the smoke, I do not forget Your statutes. ...I am small and despised, yet I do not forget Your precepts* (Psalm 119:31, 51, 61, 83, 141 NASB).

7. We keep a posture of humility and dependence, calling out to the Holy Spirit to teach us and open our spiritual eyes and ears.

> *Open my eyes, that I may behold wonderful things from Your Law. ...Incline my heart to Your testimonies, and not to dishonest gain. ...Your hands made me and fashioned me; give me understanding, so that I may learn Your commandments. ...Make Your face shine upon Your servant, and teach me Your statutes* (Psalm 119:18, 36, 73, 135 NASB).

The Evangelists

In Luke 4:18 (CSB) Jesus said, *"The Spirit of the Lord is on me, because he has anointed me to preach good news to the poor.*

He has sent me to proclaim release to the captives and recovery of sight to the blind, to set free the oppressed." This is the best passage of Scripture that reveals the heart of Jesus as the greatest evangelist who ever lived. Evangelists are graced to preach the gospel, care for the poor and needy, administer deliverance to those in bondage, and operate in miracle-working power toward those blind, oppressed, and sick in body.

Evangelists, oftentimes, feel out of place inside the house of God, and the truth is they are! Gatherings of believers often make evangelists feel bored and lethargic. They just want to go outside the four walls and win the lost. The house of God is made up of living stones who represent believers in Jesus Christ (see 1 Peter 2). The calling of evangelists is to go outside the house and collect lost stones (unbelievers) and bring them back in to be discipled by pastors and teachers. To use another example, evangelists are graced to catch the fish, not clean them. Pastors and teachers will nurse, disciple, and help those newly saved to embrace their new spiritual family. The apostles and prophets will then function to help the new convert experience revival, spiritual gifts, a revelation of Christ Jesus, and so much more. It is truly glorious when all five ministries work together, and they should!

> "It is truly glorious when all five ministries work together, and they should!"

Planting Churches

One of the greatest tragedies in America is that so many evangelists are planting churches. When they operate outside of their grace, the house of God becomes a mile wide and an inch deep. Every week, people get saved again and the church grows numerically, but in the long run it lacks deep spirituality. In other words, evangelists have a tremendous grace to win souls, cast out devils, and heal the sick, but they are not called to pastor or be a teacher. Remember when Phillip the evangelist went down to Samaria and preached the good news? Many began to be saved, healed, and delivered. But Acts 8:14-15 (NASB) says, *"Now when the apostles in Jerusalem heard that Samaria had received the word of God, they sent them Peter and John, who came down and prayed for them that they would receive the Holy Spirit."* Phillip had fulfilled his evangelistic calling to preach the good news, bind up the brokenhearted, and proclaim freedom to the captives. Once he had operated in his grace, he then headed back to Jerusalem and Peter and John, who were apostles, came to town and began their work. Notice how these men operated as a team and understood their different roles and functions! While evangelists primarily function outside the four walls of the church, they are called to inject the evangelistic ministry of Jesus inside the church to believers and help them fulfill the Great Commission. When evangelists refuse to join local churches because they feel called to the lost, broken, and needy, their marriages and families will suffer greatly.

In the new era, pastors, teachers, and evangelists are going to work together like never before. The shepherding, teaching, and evangelistic sides of Jesus Christ are going to greatly bless His body. We need a greater measure of humility and a God-given desire to work together. Dr. Michael Brown imparts a warning to all those involved in church work when he says:

> For so many today, ministry is the road to success, the way to be recognized and known by all. It means the acclaim of the crowds with the glitter and gold, the royal pastor ruling from his throne. It provides an identity in church and in the world, as though ministry made the man. We have gotten things totally wrong. Ministry does not exalt the man. Ministry means service. Ministry means being last and not first. The higher the call, the lower you must go. The grander the vision, the greater the sacrifice. And the only one to exalt is Jesus. We are to be jealous for His reputation and His reputation alone.

Note

1. John Piper, *Finally Alive* (Fearn, UK: Christian Focus Publications, 2009).

CHAPTER 9

New Era Leadership DNA

There is a hunger emerging in this generation for authentic and accountable relationships within the body of Christ like never before. This includes a desire for church leaders to be more focused on relationship than their function or title. The fivefold ministry can no longer afford to be disconnected from the very body they are called to train and equip. This inevitably will cause a massive paradigm shift in the way both leaders and saints relate to one another. I anticipate that a religious system that has modeled itself more after the Pharisees and religious leaders than Jesus Christ will rage at this new era in the body of Christ.

The New Leadership Wineskin

I recently rode in the car with a well-known minister in his early 60s. He gave me a unique perspective on this hunger for relationship and transparency. He said, "The problem with the current hunger in this generation is that they want intimate relationship, which requires too much out of church leaders. In my day, the people were satisfied with coming and watching us minister. Now the people want to get more involved, and it's too bad." As he said these words, I was overcome with grief and began to weep right in front of him. This experience as I have traveled around the world and interacted with many church leaders is not an isolated one. In fact, my heart aches and groans for so many church leaders in America and other nations (especially those in their 50s and 60s) who are set on continuing to function in an old wineskin of performance and not a new wineskin of deep love and relationship. It worked back in the day, but those days are over. An emphasis on platforms, titles, and ministry accomplishments no longer impresses, or is even the desire, among many saints today.

> **"Church leaders who refuse to learn how to actively mother and father the generations will become obsolete in the days ahead."**

I'm convinced that church leaders who refuse to learn how to actively mother and father the generations will become obsolete in the days ahead. And by obsolete, I mean out of date. I foresee many large churches shutting down and no longer being effective because they refuse to speak to the hunger that is growing like wildfire in the body of Christ.

The "old wineskin" in the Church is currently trembling because the saints are getting over the one-man-ministry-does-all model. They are looking for fathers and mothers who are willing to roll up their sleeves and do life with them. They are searching for church leaders to model healthy marriages and what it looks like for your kids to serve the Lord with everything in them.

The "old wineskin" in the Church is also confused because the saints can see through and recognize fake more than ever before. The days of plastic smiles and worshiping platform ministry are over. Living rooms and dining room tables are going to be powerful vehicles of encounter in the new era. The saints are going to be taught how to steward the presence of God in their homes before they ever try to welcome Him in a church service.

I'm prophesying to you that thousands of church leaders in the global Church are on the ropes, not sure if they can even keep going, because they have failed to recognize the new wineskin that is forming in the earth. The church leaders in the days ahead who will form the new wineskin into which God will pour out the new wine (whether they are 25 or 65 years old) will model and teach true servanthood, humility that brings honor, and deep transparency and relationship. New-era leaders will be accessible and not focused on platforms and microphones. They will place primary emphasis on the place of prayer and making disciples in one-on-one and small group settings.

A Bombshell Phone Conversation

I had a heartbreaking phone conversation six months ago with a pastor from another state. After talking about his ministry, he asked me what my plans were for the weekend. I told him my wife and I were hosting the monthly married couples gathering. We were so excited to host the thirty couples who were gathering. I told him that it was our absolute favorite gathering of the month.

He gasped on the other end of the phone. "The people in your church know where you live, Jeremiah?" he said. I admit that he totally caught me off guard. He was emphatic: "I hope you are setting boundaries between you and the people, brother. Make sure you aren't getting too close with any of the congregants or your church staff. When you build too much relationship with those you lead, they will stop honoring you. Besides, you are gaining popularity in the body of Christ and you really need to distance yourself from the people to protect the anointing on your life."

As I listened to this pastor who had been leading the congregation he pastored for more than 25 years, my heart just grieved. I hung up the phone and just wept in my house. How does distancing ourselves from the saints as church leaders look anything like the example Jesus Christ came and gave us?

At the leading of the Holy Spirit, I actually called the pastor back later that day. He was more than twice my age.

I gently said, "Brother, with all due respect, your advice to me as a young minister sounds like the Pharisees and religious leaders. Have we forgotten that one of the qualifications of being a church leader is to be hospitable? My wife and I have church members in our home three to four times a week. We see our entire church and staff we lead as a family. For us, the deeper we invest in love and relationships, the more honor we receive. I have breakfast with our elders every week and a special one-on-one with all my staff every Monday. I don't ever want to be one of those guys who has popularity and doesn't smell like sheep. I do not believe it's biblical."

There was silence on the other end of the phone. It was awkward. Then he hung up.

The Religious Hierarchy Must Fall

I truly believe the chasm that church leaders have created between themselves and the people is why so many of them are friendless, lonely, depressed, and at times suicidal. I'm convinced that the mindset and advice given to me months ago is totally old wineskin and needs to be completely abolished in all church leadership structures. I'm so brokenhearted over how many saints have never had a meal in a fivefold minister's home, never done anything fun with them, or have never known friendship with church leaders apart from ministry. I think it's totally bogus. Have we forgotten a man named Jesus Christ who came in the flesh and dwelled among the people?

The Son of God humbled Himself, taking the form of a servant and being made in the likeness of humans, and built deep love and relationship with the disciples. He chose and walked with men who betrayed and left Him in His darkest hour on the cross.

Christopher Johnson, in his book *The Fullness of Ministry*, pointedly speaks to this issue of religious hierarchy in the Church when he says:

> In the days of Jesus Christ, the scribes and Pharisees had created for themselves a hierarchy of inequality between themselves and the people. They, as spiritual leaders, created, maintained, and enjoyed the chasm of separation between themselves and the rest of God's people. They clearly viewed themselves, based upon their positions, their titles, their education, their knowledge of God's Word, and their arrogant hearts, as a different class of people than the rest. They knew nothing of deep love and relationship with those whom they were supposedly serving and leading. Is this not the same exact description of what is taking place between spiritual leaders and saints in most of the Church today?

The Emergence of House-to-House Gatherings

As we enter into this new era, a hunger for home gatherings and deep relationships will only grow. The codependence upon large buildings and the need to be entertained by a man or a woman of God is perhaps one of the number-one issues that the global pandemic has exposed in the Church. The need for parents to disciple their own children and discover the necessity of hosting the presence of God in our homes must become a major priority in the body of Christ.

These house-to-house gatherings will be marked by three primary realities—fire, family, and fathering. The fire of God was always meant to be stewarded in the context of a spiritual family with the oversight and care of fathers and mothers in the faith. Where there is fire (zeal, passion, and love) for Jesus among spiritual families (of all ages) with the protection and oversight of spiritual parenting, there will be a glory abiding upon the Church like never before. Gatherings of believers without spiritual leadership and authority are orphanages. The depth of love between the generations

> **"Fathering will heal the many wounds of so many hurting sons and daughters who do not know how to trust anymore."**

will be noticed by those in the world around us. Pure and simple-hearted devotion to Jesus Christ will mark these gatherings. Fathering will heal the many wounds of so many hurting sons and daughters who do not know how to trust anymore.

Spiritual Fathering

When Jesus said, *"Call no man your father"* (Matthew 23:9 KJV), He was not forbidding the place of spiritual fathers among His disciples. In proper context, Jesus was actually warning His disciples about the dangers of religious titles used by leaders who wanted praise and position, rather than those who humbly and lovingly served spiritual children. He was instructing His followers to avoid the kind of hypocrisy and power trip that would exalt spiritual "fathers" (and other leaders) over God as the ultimate Father. The only time having spiritual fathers is illegal in God's kingdom is when they become idols, political positions, and preeminent over God the Father. This is why Jesus could give a warning against such titles while Paul still called himself a "father" to the Corinthians (see 1 Corinthians 4:15). The difference is, Paul used the term to describe his actual relationship to the Corinthians, not to entitle himself as a leader over them.

As long as I can remember, I have always had spiritual fathers and mothers. There have consistently been older men and women in my life who have provided deep love and relationship, correction, encouragement, and accountability in every season of my life and ministry. I am currently being spiritually fathered and mothered and do not know where my marriage, family, and ministry would be without them.

Sugar Daddy or Spiritual Fathering

I have been overwhelmed recently by how many young people are reaching out to me regarding their longing for a "spiritual father." Upon engaging more than 50 of them in further conversation concerning what that looks like to them, I am becoming more convinced than ever that we have a young generation hungering for a "sugar daddy" rather than true spiritual fathering. For every cry from young people, "Where are all the true spiritual fathers?" there could be an equally valid question: "Where are all the true spiritual sons and daughters?"

People who desire a sugar daddy are looking for a one-sided relationship where they are the benefactors. In their minds, having a spiritual father means that he pours everything he has into them at no cost on their part. They are looking for a man who will teach them everything about life and faith while they sit on the couch and take notes and make no investment in him. People who are looking for a sugar daddy do not accept correction or adjustment. They do not like the idea of having to learn, serve, and honor their spiritual father for any length of time before they go back to telling him about their problems and how they have been wronged so often in life. People who want a sugar daddy instead of a true spiritual father are searching for someone who can provide for them a platform, influence, and a greater reach than they have. Their motives are impure and sometimes evil. A true spiritual father would rebuke and confront such foolishness.

Spiritual fathers, on the other hand, are men who have deposits inside of them that people admire and even desire, but you can only access the depths of the riches living on the inside of them through deep relationship and servanthood. Someone looking for a spiritual father is not looking to be served but to serve. Someone searching for a spiritual father should desire a loving leader who can bring correction and adjustment to the parts of his or her life that are immature and out of order.

> **"Someone looking for a spiritual father is not looking to be served but to serve."**

Spiritual fathers love to empower and equip. They love to challenge you and encourage you to live worthy of the call upon your life. They will faithfully remind you of the prophetic words spoken over your life and will root and ground you in the Word of God. They will listen to you, but your heart posture toward them should be quick to listen and slow to speak. My simple advice to young people searching for a true spiritual father is this: look for a man of God with whom you can build a relationship, serve him in whatever areas he needs, and make a financial investment in his life as the Holy Spirit leads. If that sounds terrible to you, then you are after a sugar daddy, not a true spiritual father. As you lay down your life, he will lay down his. Authentic relationships require time, trust, vulnerability, and sacrifice. Be patient and the fruit of a fathering relationship will come.

As we enter the new era, look for church leaders and saints to interact together much like the disciples did with Jesus. It will be missional. It will look like doing life together and ministry coming forth out of a deep heart of gratitude and love for God and brothers and sisters in Christ. Yes, there will continue to be powerful corporate gatherings and conferences in the last days, but a realm of glory has been especially reserved for living rooms and dining room tables.

CHAPTER 10

THE QUEEN OF
SHEBA PROPHECY

Several months ago, I had a prophetic dream in which I spent most of the night entering into many different gatherings. I walked into one meeting and noticed that everyone in attendance was white. Another meeting I entered was full of all African American people. Then I would go into meetings where I knew that everyone there was Democrat. I would go into other meetings where I knew everyone was Republican. Then I walked into a meeting where I knew everyone was from the Presbyterian denomination. I would go into another meeting where I knew everyone was from the Assemblies of God denomination or the Church of God denomination. I would go into other meetings where I knew that everyone was in favor of the apostolic. I then attended another meeting where I knew everyone was a fan of the pastoral. At another meeting they were discussing why the prophetic is better than the other four ministries.

I finally began to recognize in this dream that I had attended ethnic, religious, and political gatherings where the one common denominator in them all was that everyone looked like, acted like, and thought like one another. There was no variety or diversity of appearance, values, or opinions. As I was pondering the meetings I had attended, suddenly, a curtain was pulled back right in front of my face in the dream. What appeared to me in large, bright letters was the phrase, *"The disease of spiritual nepotism."* Now at the time, I really didn't know what the term *nepotism* meant, but now I do.

> **"If satan's attack is successful, everyone involved will come out of the battle hurt and wounded."**

Nepotism refers to the favoring and giving of influence to friends and family.

I immediately knew that God was going to expose the disease of spiritual nepotism in the new era. Every single gathering that I had attended earlier was simply an echo chamber. The meetings were full of people who voted the same way, believed the same doctrine, and were of the same race, and God was pointing His finger toward this practice and disease of spiritual nepotism. Favoring friends and family and gathering together because we all look alike, act alike, and talk the same, greatly displeases the heart of God.

The Queen of Sheba

The next scene in the dream brought a woman walking in whom I did not recognize but knew she was from a different time period. She was wearing beautiful clothes that looked like they were from the Middle East. In her hands, she was carrying a large vase that had many oils and spices in it. Suddenly and by way of revelation, I knew she was the Queen of Sheba! The Holy Spirit reminded me of when she came before King Solomon in 1 Kings 10:6-10 (NIV). It says:

> *She said to the king, "The report I heard in my own country about your achievements and your wisdom is true. But I did not believe these things until I came and saw with my own eyes. Indeed, not even half was told me; in wisdom and wealth you have far exceeded the report I heard. How happy your people must be! How happy your officials, who continually stand before you and hear your wisdom! Praise be to the Lord your God, who has delighted in you and placed you on the throne of Israel. Because of the Lord's eternal love for Israel, he has made you king to maintain justice and righteousness." And she gave the king 120 talents of gold, large quantities of spices, and precious stones. Never again were so many spices brought in as those the queen of Sheba gave to King Solomon.*

As I woke up from this dream, the spirit of prophecy was heavily upon me. I began to say out loud, "The spices are coming! The spices are coming!" I truly believe God is saying to the global Church that we are entering a new era when He is confronting the gatherings of believers that only include Christians who are of a certain race, denomination, or political affiliation. He is sending men and women like the Queen of Sheba who are going to bring needed spices, flavors, revelation, wisdom, and spiritual insight that many gatherings do not even realize they do not have. We need Christian gatherings that are multi-ethnic, multi-denominational, and welcome those who share a different perspective of the kingdom of God than we do.

> **"When apostles and prophets begin to work together with pastors, teachers, and evangelists, we will finally begin to see the fullness of Jesus Christ revealed, demonstrated, and manifested in the earth."**

I see gatherings full of apostles, prophets, teachers, pastors, and evangelists from every tongue, tribe, and nation. The old wineskins of jealousy, rivalry, pride, and insecurity among God's people are passing away. A new era is upon us in the global Church that will involve team leadership, houses of prayer for the nations, dining room tables, and living rooms where everyone is welcome to share their perspective on the kingdom of God. We must recognize that we will never have the full council of God in our midst unless every tongue, tribe, and nation has a place at our table. As the New Jesus People Movement explodes across the earth, may our hearts explode with joy concerning things that our ears have not heard and our eyes have not seen yet. When apostles and prophets begin to work together with pastors, teachers, and evangelists, we will finally begin to see the fullness of Jesus Christ revealed, demonstrated, and manifested in the earth. Fivefold ministers who are accessible, carry the heart of God, and walk in humility will heal the wounds of a generation that has been hurt by the Church so badly. The saints finally being equipped for the work of ministry in their own sphere of influence rather than being treated like fish in a small bowl, will lead to the greatest harvest of souls the world has ever known.

In the new era, we must be diligent to keep the unity of the Spirit and the bonds of peace. We need to always keep in mind that no matter what our differences are, there is one body, one Spirit, one Lord, one faith, one baptism, and one God and Father who is over all and through all and in all (see Ephesians 4:3-6). To the global body of Christ, I remind us that our greatest days are in front of us, not behind us. We are destined with the help of the Holy Spirit to give Jesus Christ His full inheritance in the earth. What an honor, what a joy, what a privilege to pioneer and work together in this new era. The best is yet to come!

About Jeremiah Johnson

Jeremiah and Morgan Johnson have a rich history of church planting, establishing ministries, and discipling leaders and saints. A bestselling author of multiple books and a globally recognized prophet, Jeremiah has ministered in 42 states and 25 foreign nations. He is also a popular television guest on *The 700 Club,* Daystar, TBN, Sid Roth's *It's Supernatural!, The Jim Bakker Show,* and GodTV. Morgan is a successful entrepreneur and business owner who loves investing in her family, health, and travel. She is also passionate about and loves ministering to marriages, kids, and women.

Upon graduating from Southeastern University, the Johnsons planted a church in Central Florida in 2010 and successfully pioneered Heart of the Father Ministry for a decade. As the church family multiplied, birthed a second campus over the years, and leaders were raised up, Jeremiah and Morgan passed the leadership off to a tremendous elder team who now leads the church together.

After transitioning out of their role in Florida in 2020, the Johnsons were divinely called to North Carolina through an invitation from God to birth and establish The Altar Global and The Altar School of Ministry. The Altar Global is a growing movement of Christians from around the world who share a common passion for the return of Jesus Christ and the preparation of the Bride for that glorious day. The Altar School is a one-year intensive program that carries a mandate to disciple end-time messengers in every sphere of society.

In 2022, God called the Johnsons to plant The Ark Fellowship, which serves as a local church community for many individuals, marriages, and families in the Charlotte, North Carolina, region who partner and serve The Altar Global movement and attend The Altar School.

From planting churches to traveling and ministering around the world, birthing an end-time movement, and establishing schools of ministry, the Johnsons have given their entire lives to the front lines of the kingdom of God.

For more information on The Altar Global movement go to: www.thealtarglobal.com.

For more information on The Altar School go to: www.thealtar.school

For more information on The Ark Fellowship Church go to: www.arkfellowship.church.